The Tyndale New Testament Commentaries

General Editor: PROFESSOR R. V. G. TASKER, M.A., D.D.

THE EPISTLE OF PAUL
TO THE EPHESIANS

THE EPISTLE OF PAUL
TO THE

EPHESIANS

AN INTRODUCTION AND COMMENTARY

by

FRANCIS FOULKES, M.A., B.D., M.Sc.
Principal, Vining Christian Leadership Centre,
Akure, Nigeria

LONDON
THE TYNDALE PRESS
Thirty-nine · Bedford Square · W.C.1

Printed in Great Britain by
BILLING & SONS LTD.
GUILDFORD AND LONDON

GENERAL PREFACE

ALL who are interested in the teaching and study of the New Testament today cannot fail to be concerned with the lack of commentaries which avoid the extremes of being unduly technical or unhelpfully brief. It is the hope of the editor and publishers that this present series will do something towards the supply of this deficiency. Their aim is to place in the hands of students and serious readers of the New Testament, at a moderate cost, commentaries by a number of scholars who, while they are free to make their own individual contributions, are united in a common desire to promote a truly biblical theology.

The commentaries are primarily exegetical and only secondarily homiletic, though it is hoped that both student and preacher will find them informative and suggestive. Critical questions are fully considered in introductory sections, and also, at the author's discretion, in additional notes.

The commentaries are based on the Authorized (King James) Version, partly because this is the version which most Bible readers possess, and partly because it is easier for commentators, working on this foundation, to show why, on textual and linguistic grounds, the later versions are so often to be preferred. No one translation is regarded as infallible, and no single Greek manuscript or group of manuscripts is regarded as always right! Greek words are transliterated to help those unfamiliar with the language, and to save those who do know Greek the trouble of discovering what word is being discussed.

There are many signs today of a renewed interest in what the Bible has to say and of a more general desire to understand its meaning as fully and clearly as possible. It is the hope of all those concerned with this series that God will graciously use what they have written to further this end.

R. V. G. TASKER.

CONTENTS

AUTHOR'S PREFACE

SOME of the New Testament Epistles have had few outstanding commentaries written on them in English in the past hundred years. This is not so in the case of Ephesians. Our study of this Epistle is enriched by the judicious work of Armitage Robinson, Westcott and Abbott on the Greek text, the invaluable practical expositions of Findlay and Dale, and most of all by the work of Bishop Handley Moule whose work always offers the uncommon combination of careful scholarship and devotional application. To these and others (teachers and preachers as well as writers) I have been indebted constantly, and I realize that this has been the case often where I have not been sufficiently aware of the source of my indebtedness to acknowledge it.

In the Introduction there is some attempt to study briefly the problems associated with the peculiar nature of Ephesians, the Epistle's relationship to other New Testament writings, its authorship and original destination. These questions, however, interesting as they are, appear to be less important for the understanding of this Epistle, than is the case with almost any other New Testament letter. Therefore, I do not regard the Introduction as the most important part of the book. Doctrinal teaching is given in the Epistle without the direct application to the problems of a particular situation which we find in an Epistle such as Galatians; we have moral precepts without that reference to the peculiar problems of a church which we have in the Corinthian Epistles. Therefore, it is the study of the language and thought of the Epistle itself that will lead us most deeply into the writer's understanding of the glory of God in Christ and of the high calling of those who themselves have come to live in Him. Sir Edwyn Hoskyns once asked, 'Can we study a language, and awake to the Truth? Can we bury ourselves in a lexicon, and arise in the presence of God?'

9

Many have found that they can indeed in the case of the words of this Epistle, which Coleridge called 'one of the divinest compositions of man'.

FRANCIS FOULKES.

CHIEF ABBREVIATIONS

AV — English Authorized Version (King James).

LXX — Septuagint Version.

NEB — New English Bible, 1961.

RSV — American Revised Standard Version, 1946.

RV — English Revised Version, 1881.

Abbott — *Ephesians and Colossians* (The International Critical Commentaries) by T. K. Abbott, 1899.

Allan — *Commentary on Ephesians* (The Torch Bible Commentaries) by J. A. Allan, 1959.

Barclay — *Commentary on Galatians and Ephesians* (The Daily Study Bible) by William Barclay, 1954.

Barry — 'The Epistles to the Ephesians, Philippians, and Colossians' by A. Barry in *A New Testament Commentary for English Readers*, ed. C. J. Ellicott, 1896.

BDB — *A Hebrew and English Lexicon of the Old Testament* by F. Brown, S. R. Driver and C. A. Briggs, 1907.

Bruce — *The Epistle to the Ephesians* by F. F. Bruce, 1961.

Calvin — *Commentary on Galatians and Ephesians* by John Calvin, translated by W. Pringle, 1957.

Dale — *The Epistle to the Ephesians* by R. W. Dale, 1883.

Findlay — *Commentary on Ephesians* (The Expositor's Bible) by G. G. Findlay, 1902.

Lock — *Commentary on Ephesians* (The Westminster Commentaries) by W. Lock, 1929.

LS — *A Greek–English Lexicon* by H. G. Liddell and R. Scott.

Mitton — *The Epistle to the Ephesians* by C. L. Mitton, 1951.

Moffatt	*A New Translation of the Bible* by J. Moffatt, 1913.
Moule (*CB*)	*Commentary on Ephesians* (The Cambridge Bible for Schools and Colleges) by H. C. G. Moule, 1884.
Moule (*ES*)	*Ephesians Studies* by H. C. G. Moule, 1900.
Murray	*Commentary on Ephesians* (The Cambridge Greek Testament) by J. O. F. Murray, 1914.
Phillips	*The New Testament in Modern English* by J. B. Phillips, 1958.
Robinson	*St. Paul's Epistle to the Ephesians*[2] by J. Armitage Robinson, 1904.
Simpson	*The Epistles to the Ephesians and Colossians* (New London Commentary) by E. K. Simpson and F. F. Bruce, 1958.
Scott	*Commentary on the Epistles to Colossians, Philemon and Ephesians* (Moffatt New Testament Commentary) by E. F. Scott, 1930.
Westcott	*Saint Paul's Epistle to the Ephesians* by B. F. Westcott, 1906.
Weymouth	*The New Testament in Modern Speech* by R. F. Weymouth, 1903.

INTRODUCTION

I. THE NATURE AND TEACHING OF THE EPISTLE

AS we begin to read the Epistle to the Ephesians, we find that it opens in the same way as the other New Testament letters that we recognize as Paul's: 'Paul, an apostle of Jesus Christ by the will of God, to the saints . . .' As we continue, however, we find many features that make it stand out as different from all the others. In the first place, apart from the fact that it speaks of Paul as privileged to be a minister of the gospel of the grace of Christ (iii. 2–13), and in consequence of his ministry imprisoned (iii. 1, iv. i, vi. 20), and of Tychicus as the bearer of the letter (vi. 21f.), there are no other personal references, no greetings, no reminiscences, no messages to or from individuals such as have so large a place in the other letters which we know as Paul's. Furthermore, there are apparently no specific problems, either doctrinal or practical, that have given rise to this Epistle, and have to be dealt with in it, whereas all the other Pauline letters[1] are written to deal with particular issues and definite situations that we can assess from the Epistles themselves.

In many respects Ephesians reads more like a sermon—in some parts more like a prayer or a mighty doxology—than a letter written to meet some special need in a church or group of churches. It is like a sermon on the greatest and widest theme possible for a Christian sermon—the eternal purpose of God, which He is fulfilling through His Son Jesus Christ, and working out in and through the Church. One thought leads on to another all the way through the Epistle without constant reference to the situation of the readers. Chapters i–iii are principally the doctrinal elaboration of the great theme, and chapters iv–vi teach what should be the practical con-

[1] For the purposes of this Introduction those Epistles which bear the name of Paul will be referred to as the Pauline Epistles.

sequences of it for human life and relationships. There is, however, no clear-cut division between doctrine and ethics, but rather an intimate linking of the two throughout.

It has sometimes been said that we have doctrine in this Epistle such as we find nowhere else in the Pauline letters. The bearing of this question upon the matter of authorship will be dealt with more fully later. But, without prejudging that issue, we would say that we have here all the great doctrines of the Christian faith that we find embedded in other Pauline letters, but whereas in them they are dealt with as they bear on the particular problems that the apostle is meeting in the life of the churches to which he is writing, here they are developed in such a way as helps to expound the great theme of this whole Epistle, the purpose of God in Christ for His Church. We may see this best by examining briefly some of the cardinal doctrines.

First, let us take the teaching of reconciliation through the cross of Christ. The work of the cross is shown to be for our redemption, for the forgiveness of our sins (i. 7, ii. 13, 16; cf. Rom. v. 6–10; 1 Cor. xv. 3; Col. i. 14), that we might become the children of God and heirs of God's kingdom (i. 5, 18; cf. Rom. viii. 14–17; Gal. iii. 26, iv. 5–7). We have a clear, typically Pauline statement of the doctrine of justification by faith: 'by grace are ye saved through faith; and that not of yourselves: it is the gift of God: not of works, lest any man should boast' (ii. 8f.; cf. Rom. iii. 21–26; Gal. ii. 16, iii. 11, 24f.)—though to it is added emphatically the further purpose, 'We are his workmanship, created in Christ Jesus unto good works, which God hath before ordained that we should walk in them' (ii. 10). Then, most important of all, after it has been stated that He has made peace by the blood of the cross, that those who were dead in sin might receive new life (ii. 1ff.; cf. Rom. v. 12–21, vi. 21–23), and have access to God (cf. Rom. v. 1f.), it is added that the cross is also the way of peace between man and man, the means of the breaking down of the middle wall of partition between Jew and Gentile, the instrument for killing the old enmity between them. So it can be said that because Christ came to bring peace, now 'through

14

him we both have access by one Spirit unto the Father' (ii. 18). This same emphasis on the cross as the means of unity in the fellowship of the Church is also seen in the way that this Epistle speaks of the apostolic privilege of the ministry of the gospel. We are accustomed to Paul's speaking of the privilege of preaching the gospel, and in particular of being called to evangelize the Gentiles (e.g. Rom. i. 13–16, xi. 13, xv. 15–20; Gal. i. 15f., ii. 9; Col. i. 24–29); but in this letter there is the further emphasis on the apostle's calling and privilege to communicate to others the 'mystery', the great revealed secret of the faith, 'that the Gentiles are fellow-heirs, and fellow-members of the body' (iii. 6, RV).

In teaching concerning the resurrection and exaltation of Christ we have the truth presented in a way that is familiar to us from other Pauline Epistles (i. 20–22; cf. Phil. ii. 9–11; Col. i. 15–18). But here in Ephesians the climax of the statement of the exaltation of Christ is that God 'gave him to be the head over all things to the church, which is his body, the fulness of him that filleth all in all' (i. 22f.). It is the purpose of God that men who were dead in trespasses and sins should be raised up together with Christ (cf. Rom. vi. 3–11; Col. ii. 12, iii. 1–3), and with Christ be made to sit in the heavenly places (Eph. ii. 5f.); but the treatment of the resurrection and exaltation in this Epistle goes further than this. He has 'ascended up far above all heavens, that he might fill all things', and that He might so give gifts to His Church that it might grow 'unto the measure of the stature of the fulness of Christ' (iv. 9–16).

We have also typically Pauline teaching about the Holy Spirit. It is by the Spirit that God indwells those who believe in Christ (ii. 22, iii. 16f., v. 18; cf. Rom. viii. 9–11; 1 Cor. iii. 16, vi. 19); the Spirit is the 'seal' and 'earnest' given them by God (i. 13f., iv. 30; cf. Rom. viii. 23; 2 Cor. i. 22, v. 5). He helps them in prayer (vi. 18; cf. Rom. viii. 26f.), and is the means not only of access to God (ii. 18) but of wisdom in the things of God and enlightenment in the practical details of life (i. 8, 17, iii. 5; cf. 1 Cor. ii. 10–13). Again, however, the teaching of the work of the Spirit finds its greatest development in connection with the Church and its unity. The unity of the Church is 'the unity of the Spirit' (iv. 3); the Spirit is the Giver of the gifts that the Church needs for its growth (iv. 7ff.; cf. 1 Cor. xii. 4–11), and the goal of the use of these gifts in their diversity is 'the unity of the faith', the development of the Church in all its members 'unto a perfect man'.

What has been said already about other doctrines is sufficient indication of the great place that the doctrine of the Church has in this Epistle. But the difference between this and other Pauline Epistles is one of emphasis and of degree rather than of essential teaching. There is little or nothing here that is new, but we have a greater emphasis on the universal Church and its unity, and a greater variety of ways of expressing the purpose of the Church than we have in any other Pauline letter. The writer's mind is manifestly filled with the sense of the mighty purpose of God for His Church. He speaks, as we have seen, of the exaltation of Christ, and the climax of it all is His headship of the Church which is His Body (i. 22f.; cf. 1 Cor. xii. 27; Col. i. 18, 24, ii. 17). He speaks of the reconciliation of men not only to God but to one another, and emphasizes that this is in the Church, 'the household of God' (ii. 19; cf. Gal. vi. 10), the temple built on the foundation of the apostles and prophets (ii. 21; cf. 1 Cor. iii. 16; 2 Cor. vi. 16) that is God's habitation in the Spirit. We have noted what the writer says in chapter iv about the Church and Christian unity. He goes on to deal with the very different subject of Christian marriage, taking as an illustration the Old Testament figure of the people of God as the bride (cf. 2 Cor. xi. 2), and thereby expresses great truths about the relationship of the Lord to His Church. Finally we should note the cosmic significance that he gives to the Church. It has a great divine purpose in the world, to proclaim Christ and bring men into unity in Him; but it has an eternal purpose, a task which is not completed in this world and in this age—to make known 'unto the principalities and powers in heavenly places' what is 'the manifold wisdom of God' (iii. 10f.).

It is thus fair to say that the doctrine of this Epistle is essentially Pauline, but developed along such lines as are necessary in the task of expounding the great theme of the whole letter. It immediately occurs to us to ask why this letter, unlike the others, should be concerned with pure doctrine and ethics, unrelated to any particular situation? Why is its form so different from that of the others? What was the occasion of the writing of a letter such as this? The next important stage in the consideration of these questions must be an attempt to answer a further question: Is the title 'to the Ephesians' the real and original title?

II. DESTINATION

From the second century this Epistle was received almost universally under the title 'to the Ephesians'. But there is evidence that the title is not truly original, and is, at least to some extent, a misnomer. The oldest manuscript of Ephesians that we possess, the Chester Beatty papyrus of about AD 200, and the great fourth-century codices Sinaiticus and Vaticanus, and certain other authorities do not have the words 'at Ephesus' in i. 1. Marcion, notorious for his heretical teachings in the mid-second century, refers to this letter as the epistle to the Laodiceans. This may have been because he had a copy with 'at Laodicea' inserted in i. 1, or, more probably, it was a deduction from the reference to the letter 'from Laodicea' in Colossians iv. 16. At least there are no obvious doctrinal reasons why he should have said it was written to people other than the Ephesians if such was the original title. The evidence is complicated at this point in that the second-century Muratorian Fragment on the Canon refers to two epistles, one to the Ephesians and one to the Laodiceans; but when we come to the third century we find the great biblical scholar Origen saying that the words 'at Ephesus' were not in the manuscripts that he knew. Tertullian, about the same time, accused the Marcionites of tampering with the title, but he made no reference to the text. Basil and Jerome in the fourth century make it plain that the best manuscripts they had did not include the words.

If we could think of the Epistle without these words in i. 1

and without a title, we would have to admit that there is no clear evidence from the contents of the letter that it was sent to Ephesus, and a good deal that suggests that it could hardly have been addressed simply to the church in that city. For three years Paul had lived and worked in Ephesus (Acts xix and xx. 31). When in particular we consider the very moving way in which Paul addressed the elders of the church of Ephesus in Acts xx. 18–35, we may well ask whether he could have written a letter to this church without reference to the time he spent there, without mention of individuals whom he knew so well in the church, and with no personal news of any kind. Instead the letter was written as if many, at least, of his readers were not well known to its author (i. 15, iii. 2, iv. 20f.). The evidence of the nature of the Epistle as a whole strongly supports the textual evidence of i. 1 that this letter could hardly be a message written by the apostle Paul simply for his many friends and converts in the church of Ephesus.

Thus there are two questions that we must try to answer. To whom was the Epistle written? and, How did it come to be known as the Epistle of Paul the apostle to the Ephesians? Neither can be answered with certainty, but there are a number of suggestions that have been made.

a. It was not sent to a particular church, but to any Christians who might read it. Some have argued that i. 1 makes sense without the words 'at Ephesus' or any similar place reference, reading 'the saints who are also faithful in Christ Jesus'. This is very difficult grammatically; 'faithful' is hardly an expression that, added to 'saints', requires such emphasis as is given by the article, participle and the linking 'and' together (*tois ousin kai*). The parallels in Romans 1 and 2 Corinthians and Philippians point almost inevitably to the conclusion that there was originally a place-name in the verse. Moreover, there are passages that obviously were written with specific readers in mind, even if they were readers in a number of different churches (i. 15ff., vi. 21f.).

b. It was sent to a particular church, but the address and personal greetings were later omitted so that the letter might have a more general use. It then happened to become attached particularly to Ephesus. The greatest difficulty about this suggestion is that in most of Paul's letters there are marks all the way through of the situation and the people to whom they were addressed. We could not remove the marks of the destination merely by removing the greetings and the address. This fact stands in particular against the view of Marcion that the Epistle was sent to Laodicea. It may be added that Colossians iv. 16 speaks of a letter 'from Laodicea' and not simply 'to Laodicea', and indeed Paul would hardly have given greetings to particular Christians at Laodicea in Colossians iv. 15 if he had been writing another letter to them at the same time.

c. It was sent to a number of churches in a particular area, probably the Roman province of Asia. Internal and external evidence provide much to support this view. There are two forms of this suggestion. One copy of the letter, it is supposed, was taken round to the different churches, and a gap was left for the bearer to fill in the name as he went. Against this it has been argued that such an expedient cannot be paralleled in ancient letter-writing, but the answer can be given that 'so simple and common sense a plan does not require to be justified by precedents'.[1] Alternatively, it is suggested that there were a number of copies of the letter each bearing a different place-name. The copy addressed to Ephesus then became the letter accepted, because Ephesus was the most important church. If this were the case, however, it is strange that there is no trace of any other place-name in the manuscripts that have come down to us. The most cogent objection to the view that the Epistle was written to a group of churches in the Roman province of Asia is that we have several New Testament writings that were sent to a group of churches— 2 Corinthians, Galatians, 1 Peter, Revelation—but in each case the fact is made clear in their introductions. Why could not these churches of Asia have been addressed in such a way? We cannot give an answer to this question, except to say that the idea of a messenger putting in a different place-name as

[1] E. Graham on Ephesians in *A New Commentary on Holy Scripture*, ed. Gore, Goudge and Guillaume (1928).

he reached each of the churches is a not impossible alternative as a manner of addressing them all.

d. Lastly, it has been argued by many in recent years that this strange uncertainty about the destination of the Epistle, considered together with other peculiar features of the letter, provides evidence in support of the hypothesis that Paul himself did not write Ephesians, but that it came from the hand of another after the apostle himself had died. To this issue of authorship we must now turn, but before we attempt to give any verdict we must first consider the relation of Ephesians to certain other New Testament writings.

III. EPHESIANS AND COLOSSIANS

Without fear of contradiction it may be said that there are more numerous and more sustained similarities between Ephesians and Colossians than between any other two New Testament Epistles. It is said that, with varying degrees of similarity, 75 of the 155 verses of Ephesians are found in Colossians. There are different categories in which the parallels between the two Epistles should be considered.

The plan and argument of the Epistles are similar. Both begin with a doctrinal section that shows forth the glory of Christ and the grandeur of His purpose; both proceed to apply this to personal life, and both move on to similar exhortations concerning human relationships. Within this framework there are whole sections that are very much alike. In the early part of the letters (i. 15ff. and Col. i. 3ff.), in similar but by no means identical language, Paul gives thanks for the readers and prays for them; but admittedly this is a feature common to many of the Pauline Epistles. Of more significance is the way in which both deal with Christian living, speaking of putting off the old man, and putting on the new (iv. 17ff. and Col. iii. 5ff.). The 'walk' of the Christian is dealt with in both letters, the duty of thanksgiving, and its expression in praise and song (v. 15ff. and Col. iii. 16f., iv. 5f.). There is a close similarity in the instructions to husbands and wives, to parents and children, slaves and masters, though the

Ephesians passage (v. 22–vi. 9) is fuller than that in Colossians (iii. 18–iv. 1). In the writer's request for prayer for himself, there is in both cases a reference to his bonds, and to the mystery of the gospel to be made known (vi. 18–20 and Col. iv. 3f.), and there is a similarity also in earlier references to the apostle's commission to make known the mystery of the gospel (iii. 1–13 and Col. i. 23–29). The parallels cannot be coincidental, but they are not such as one would find where a writer was dependent on another written record before him. They can only be explained by the assumption that the mind of the writer of Ephesians was full of the thought and expression of Colossians.

Furthermore, both in the sections already referred to, and also virtually throughout the two letters, there are many parallels in expression, parallels more numerous than we find between any other Pauline Epistles, parallels which demand an explanation in terms of some special connection between Ephesians and Colossians. It is impossible to deal with these parallels here, but a few examples can be taken.[1] In the following cases we have words or expressions that are not found in other Pauline Epistles, but are in both Ephesians and Colossians: the fullness of God or of Christ (i. 23, iii. 19, iv. 13; Col. i. 19, ii. 9); alienation from God or from His people (ii. 12, iv. 18; Col. i. 21); redeeming the time (v. 16; Col. iv. 5); being rooted in Christ or in His love (iii. 17; Col. ii. 7); redemption specifically interpreted as 'the forgiveness of sins' (i. 7; Col. i. 14); the word of the truth of the gospel (i. 13; Col. i. 5); forbearing one another (iv. 2; Col. iii. 13); covetousness defined as idolatry (v. 5; Col. iii. 5); forgiving one another even as the Lord has forgiven (iv. 32; Col. iii. 13); the joints of the body being knit together and the increase of the body in consequence (iv. 16; Col. ii. 19).

What we have said already of the relation between the doctrine of Ephesians and that of the other Pauline Epistles is true in a special sense of Colossians. It seems as if the great doctrinal statements of Colossians are assumed, and then there is built on them those doctrines which are the special

---

[1] For a classification of the parallels see Mitton, pp. 28off.

emphasis of this letter. In Colossians we have a great exposition of the place of Christ in the universe; this is assumed in Ephesians, but this Epistle goes further to show the cosmic significance of the Church in fulfilling the great work of Christ. In Colossians there is emphasis on the reconciliation of men to God through the cross of Christ. In Ephesians, as we have seen, this is taken for granted, and we have the further truth of the reconciliation of men one to another through the cross in the Body of Christ which is the fellowship of reconciliation.

Finally we must notice the references to Tychicus as bearer. In the parallel passages that we have noted in the two letters, there are hardly ever more than a few words in succession that are identical. The exception to this is the reference to Tychicus at the end of each letter. Mitton (p. 59) points out that here we have twenty-nine words in agreement between Ephesians and Colossians. Here is the only strong case for literary dependence (vi. 21f.; Col. iv. 7f.), and we seem forced to the conclusion that either the same writer wrote the two together or else one writer for some special reason copied the words of the other.

This particular parallel needs further consideration, but apart from that we must say that the similarities between Colossians and Ephesians are such that they cannot be accounted for by saying that one is copied from the other. On the other hand, the parallels are so extensive and detailed that they cannot be explained as stemming from the common language of the early Church, or even simply as coming from the mind of the same author. Whatever conclusions we may reach about authorship, there is manifestly a special connection between the two Epistles. For a very long time it was accepted that the explanation of the features we have described was simply that Paul wrote the two letters at about the same time. He wrote the letter to the Colossians to meet a particular situation and danger in the church at Colossae. Then with his mind still working over the theme of the greatness and glory of Christ, but moving on to consider the place of the Church in the purpose of God, he wrote Ephesians, this time without the limitation of any polemical aims. The greater measure of identity between vi. 21f. and Colossians iv. 7f. could be accounted for by the supposition that the apostle wrote the two conclusions together, when both letters had been written and were about to be despatched. In the last hundred years, however, the Pauline authorship of Ephesians has been vigorously challenged, and it has been argued that the similarities (and differences) between Colossians and Ephesians, as well as a number of other features of Ephesians, are best accounted for by the view that Paul did not write Ephesians, but that someone else, whose mind was full of the thought and expression of Paul's letters, and especially of Colossians, wrote at a later date in his name and imitating his work.

The investigation of this view requires a more careful consideration of the nature of the similarities between the Epistles than we have so far made. Opponents of Pauline authorship have pointed out, in particular, that although there is a great similarity in the words and phrases used, at times the same word or expression is used with a very different connotation. For example, although the same word 'mystery' is one of the key words of both letters, in Colossians (i. 27) the 'mystery' is 'Christ in you, the hope of glory', in Ephesians it is that the Gentiles are fellow-heirs with the Jews (iii. 3, 6). In Colossians (i. 20) reconciliation is between men and God, whereas in Ephesians it refers to the harmony of Jews and Gentiles in the one Body of Christ (ii. 16). In Colossians (ii. 10) Christ is spoken of as the 'head (*kephalē*) of all principality and power', while Ephesians (iv. 15) speaks of Him as Head of the Church. (But here we should note that Colossians also (in i. 18) speaks of Him as Head of the Church.) Then there is the word *oikonomia* which AV translates as 'dispensation', a word used only once in the New Testament other than in Ephesians and Colossians; in Colossians i. 25 it is argued that it has the sense of stewardship, or an assignment given to a steward from God, but in Ephesians i. 10 and iii. 2 it is rather a plan or arrangement of God that the word connotes. (It must be admitted, however, that the use in Ephesians iii. 2 is very like that in Colossians.) Then we may compare the expression of Colossians iii. 14, 'love, which is the bond of perfectness' (RV), with that of Ephesians iv. 3 'the bond of peace'.

Some have concluded that the same person could not have written both Epistles because differences of such a kind would not be found in the same writer. This very phenomenon of little differences and great similarities has, however, seemed to others most strongly to support the conclusion of Pauline authorship. Barry, for example, observing that 'the similarity is almost always mingled with clear and characteristic difference, marking an independent coincidence' and that 'identical expressions occur again and again in entirely different contexts, and in different degrees of prominence', argues: 'These are exactly the phenomena we may expect when two letters are written at the same time to churches neither wholly identical nor wholly dissimilar in character, and under the guidance of distinct, yet complementary, ideas. They are wholly incompatible with dependence or deliberate copyism.' A more careful study of particular words and phrases than we can give here is necessary in order to make a fair judgment. Some of the expressions are studied from this point of view within their context in the Commentary proper (e.g. see on iii. 4 for 'mystery'). We may only note here that in many cases the use of terms in the two Epistles differs in precisely the same kind of way as we have found their doctrine to differ.

Mitton (pp. 65–67) argues further, from his careful comparison of the two Epistles, that frequently one Ephesians passage corresponds to two passages in Colossians (e.g. i. 7 and Col. i. 14, 20; i. 15f. and Col. i. 4, 9); the reason for this he alleges to be that the later writer automatically linked in his mind two Colossians passages with which he was very familiar. Mitton's argument could fully be met only by a second analysis as careful as his own. It does seem, however, that it could be countered by a number of examples where there are two Ephesians passages that correspond to one in Colossians (e.g. iii. 7, 17 and Col. i. 23; i. 4, ii. 16 and Col. i. 21f.; i. 10, ii. 13f. and Col. i. 20). At least there is no decisive argument concerning authorship here; but in justice to Mitton it must be said that he considers the matter alongside what he believes to be a similar phenomenon found when Ephesians is compared with other Pauline Epistles. To such a comparison we must now turn.

IV. EPHESIANS AND OTHER NEW TESTAMENT WRITINGS

a. *Other Pauline Epistles*

Comparison of Ephesians with other Pauline writings reveals certain features which have been taken as evidence against the Pauline authorship of the Epistle. Mitton, for example, finds three such features. In the first place he sees a conflation of the content of passages from other Epistles in Ephesians, as we have noted already in his argument about the relationship with Colossians. Nothing but an equally detailed argument could answer that of Mitton, but once again it is possible to find examples where there might be said to be two Ephesians passages conflated in another Epistle.

A second argument of his in fact involves such a parallelism between one passage of another Pauline Epistle and two or more passages in Ephesians. Mitton feels that when we compare Ephesians with other Pauline letters, we do not find the kind of similarity we would expect if the same writer were drawing upon his own mind, and therefore inevitably repeating some of his earlier thoughts and expressions (i.e. we do not find the sort of similarity that we do have between other Pauline Epistles); but, rather, that certain great Pauline passages are uppermost in the mind of the writer of Ephesians. There are sustained parallels, he says, to the 'purple passages' of Paul's writings; cf. Romans i. 21–24 and Ephesians iv. 17–19; Romans iii. 20–iv. 2 and Ephesians i. 7, 19, ii. 5, 8; Romans v. 1f. and Ephesians ii. 17, 18, iii. 11f.; Romans viii. 9–39 and Ephesians i. 4–7, 11, 13f., 21, iii. 6, 16, 18f.; and he cites also other examples. It can be seen that this argument could be taken against his 'conflation' theory. We would not wish to deny the existence of noteworthy parallels between Ephesians passages and the 'purple passages' of Romans, 1 and 2 Corinthians, Galatians, Philippians and

1 Thessalonians. Rather, in that Ephesians, unlike the other letters, does not deal with particular problems, we would expect the Epistle's closest parallels to be with the great doctrinal passages of those letters, and this is the case. We would expect Ephesians to resemble most closely those Epistles which have greater doctrinal sections than the others (e.g. Romans and Colossians), and this is the case. We would expect to find that Ephesians, if it were a letter of pure Pauline doctrine and ethics without local references, had a greater number of verses or expressions in common with other Pauline Epistles than would one of the letters which abound in local references. This again is undeniably the case.

A third argument that Mitton puts forward against Pauline authorship is this fact that 88% of Ephesians is paralleled in the other Epistles, whereas the percentage of convincing parallels between any other letter and the rest is much lower. We cannot, however, reach a conclusion simply from numbers. Subject-matter and the varying length of the Epistles must be considered. The fact that Paul writes his other letters with specific local problems and situations in mind automatically reduces the likelihood of overlap in their vocabulary. In the case of Ephesians, however, his main theme is the doctrinal and practical implications of the redeeming purpose of God in Christ, a theme upon which he bases his specific injunctions in the other Epistles, and which for this reason makes reiteration of words and phrases found in other letters more likely. From this comparison with other Pauline Epistles, inconclusive from the standpoint of authorship, we must now turn to the comparison of our Epistle with non-Pauline writings in the New Testament.

We shall consider in turn different New Testament writings, and in each case try to see if there is any evidence of direct literary dependence, or if in other ways we can find features that give any indication of the probable date of the writing of Ephesians.

b. 1 Peter

There are some important parallels between 1 Peter and Ephesians. The opening doxologies are similar (but that of 2 Corinthians i. 3ff. is not dissimilar); and the treatments of the relations of husbands and wives, masters and slaves are alike (v. 22–33, vi. 5–9; 1 Pet. ii. 18–iii. 7); but the parallel in this case is not as close as that between 1 Peter and Colossians. There are also parallels in what is said of the exaltation of Christ and the subjection to Him of all the powers (i. 20f.; 1 Pet. iii. 22); in references to the Christian warfare (vi. 10ff.; 1 Pet. v. 8f.), to the gospel as hidden before but now made clear, and to its communication to angels (iii. 5f., 10; 1 Pet. i. 10ff.), to the purpose of God before the foundation of the world (i. 4; 1 Pet. i. 19f.), to the lusts of the flesh and the children of obedience and disobedience (ii. 2f.; 1 Pet. i. 14, ii. 11), to putting away guile and evil speaking (iv. 25, 31; 1 Pet. ii. 1), and to the people of God's own possession (i. 14; 1 Pet. ii. 9). We have the word *eusplanchnoi* for 'tender-hearted' used in the New Testament only in iv. 32 and 1 Peter iii. 8. Many of the likenesses are sufficiently accounted for by the general similarity of the language used by different writers in the early Church to speak of Christian teaching and conduct. An even more satisfactory explanation of the close parallels is given in the theory of Archbishop Carrington, developed by Selwyn, that there were certain standard forms that the catechetical teaching of the Church was taking even at this early stage.[1] If there is often a closer resemblance between 1 Peter and Ephesians than between 1 Peter and Colossians, the reason could well be that in Colossians there is of necessity an adaptation of the catechetical teaching to a particular situation, whereas in Ephesians this is not necessary. Various theories of literary dependence, of Ephesians on 1 Peter or *vice versa*, have been put forward, but it is hard to argue at all conclusively for such dependence, as the inability of the

---

[1] P. Carrington, *The Primitive Christian Catechism* (1940), and E. G. Selwyn, *The First Epistle of St. Peter* (1949), pp. 363ff. See also the Tyndale Commentary on 1 Peter, pp. 45ff.

exponents of these theories to agree on the direction of the borrowing evidently shows.

c. *Luke and Acts*

Similarities have also been pointed out between Ephesians and Luke and Acts. There is in Ephesians (i. 20, iv. 8–10) the same emphasis on the ascension and exaltation of Christ that we find in Luke and Acts (see Lk. xxiv. 51; Acts i. 9; and Acts ii. 32–36, vii. 55), but we also find this in other Pauline Epistles, and in any case it is a matter of basic doctrine. The references to the 'good pleasure' of God (i. 5; Lk. ii. 14), to the goal of the work of Christ as holiness and righteousness (iv. 24; Lk. i. 75), to the contrast between light and darkness (v. 8–13; Lk. xi. 33–36; Acts xxvi. 18), to the girding of the loins (vi. 14; Lk. xii. 35), have all been taken as arguments for literary dependence, but their use in the early Church must have been more general than would allow us to argue for literary dependence from this slight evidence. For this same reason no argument can be based on the fact that the expression 'filled with the Spirit' (v. 18), so common in the Lucan writings, is found in Ephesians only of the Pauline Epistles. Much has been made of the close similarities between Ephesians and the address to the Ephesian elders in Acts xx— e.g. the reference to the 'counsel' (*boulē*) of God, to lowliness, to the ministry of the grace of God. But if Ephesians is the work of the apostle, and Luke gave a substantially accurate account of Paul's address to the Ephesian elders, this is what we would expect; and this explanation is at least as likely as the theory that a later writer made use of what had already been written by Luke in Acts xx. Rather than suggesting literary dependence, the parallels tend to give a ring of truth to both.

d. *The Johannine literature*

The Johannine literature must also be considered briefly, as it has been said that in Ephesians we have Pauline teaching and expression influenced also by Johannine theology and terminology. Moffatt says that the writer of Ephesians saw breathing the atmosphere in which the Johannine literature took shape. It is true that there is a stronger emphasis on realized eschatology than in other Pauline letters. There is a common use of some of the Johannine keywords, 'light' and 'darkness', 'life' and 'death', 'love', 'knowledge', etc. There is an emphasis on the unity of the Church in Ephesians which is more like John xvii than anything in the other Pauline Epistles. There is frequent reference to the Christian finding his life 'in Christ' (cf. Jn. xv. 1–7), to Christ's indwelling His Church (iii. 17; Jn. xiv. 20, xv. 4–7) and cleansing and sanctifying it (v. 26; Jn. xv. 3, xvii. 17, 19; 1 Jn. i. 7), to the descent and ascent of Christ (iv. 9; Jn. iii. 13, 31, vii. 39), to Jesus as beloved of the Father (i. 6; Jn. iii. 35, x. 17, xv. 9, xvii. 23–26). Once again, however, literary dependence cannot be argued. The question of date may be raised (see below on this), but nearly all of the parallels mentioned involve expressions whose use can be illustrated from Christian writings earlier than the Johannine literature.

There are also particular parallels noted between Ephesians and Revelation, as well as those of the kind just mentioned. There is reference to the apostles and prophets as foundations of the Church (ii. 20, iii. 5; Rev. x. 7, xviii. 20, xxi. 14), to refusing to have fellowship with evil (v. 11; Rev. xviii. 4), to the Church as the bride of Christ (v. 25ff.; Rev. xix. 7, xxi. 2, 9, xxii. 17), to sitting in heavenly places with Christ (ii. 6; Rev. iii. 21), to the symbol of the seal (i. 13, iv. 30; Rev. vii. 2f.). In none of these cases, however, is the language and thought peculiar to Ephesians and Revelation, nor can they be taken to support any argument on the dating of Ephesians.

e. Hebrews

A comparison of Ephesians and Hebrews reveals certain similar doctrines stressed in both: redemption through Christ, the cleansing of the Church, the exaltation of Christ, and our access to the Father through Him; but we can hardly base any argument for authorship or date on this.

That there are marked parallels between Ephesians and

these non-Pauline writings cannot be denied. Two things, however, need to be said. A good number, at least, of the parallels listed are common also to other Pauline Epistles and these writings. Then also the fact that Ephesians has more New Testament parallels than do the other Epistles, can be explained adequately by the fact that Ephesians is not a controversial writing, and we would naturally expect more overlap where the common Christian vocabulary used in preaching and teaching is involved, than where particular problems are treated. This Epistle, if Paul's, is, moreover, one of his latest and most mature works, and it could fairly readily be established in argument that there are greater similarities between the non-Pauline writings considered above and the later Pauline letters than between them and Paul's earlier Epistles. We may well ask whether the similarities between Ephesians and these various writings are not simply eloquent testimony to the great and increasing measure of unanimity in the early Christian preaching and teaching, whether in Asia, Rome, Ephesus or Antioch, whether from the lips of Peter, Paul, John or any other. Nowhere are the similarities such as to make direct dependence (as there manifestly is between 2 Peter and Jude) a necessary deduction, nor yet such as to make some special connection (as between Ephesians and Colossians) appear inevitable.

V.   ARGUMENTS FOR A LATER DATE

Apart from the question of the similarity of Ephesians to other New Testament writings, it is argued that there are signs in the Epistle itself which indicate that it was written at a date later than Paul's death.

It has been argued, in particular, that Paul spent most of his life striving for the equality of Jews and Gentiles in the Church. Could he have written, as appears the case in Ephesians, as if this controversy was settled, and required no further argument? But for Paul it *was* settled, as his argument in Romans (with the polemic of Galatians removed) itself shows. He does not argue elsewhere that it was the object of the work of Christ in His cross to bring Jews and Gentiles into one, but that could well have been a natural result of his further meditation on the work of Christ and the unity of the Church. The task of the Church in working out the purpose of God is basic to this Epistle, and this accounts for the way in which the question of Jews and Gentiles is treated. Justification by faith is not the primary argument, as in Romans and Galatians; therefore here the meaning of the death of Christ can be related most prominently to the realization of peace both between men and God and between man and man. The reasons for the past division between Jew and Gentile are not vital in the way that they were at the time of the writing of Galatians, and so the realization of the union of the two can be treated as an illustration (indeed to Paul the most noteworthy illustration) of the unity that Christ brings. Findlay (pp. 5f.) argues strongly that it would be hard for anyone other than the apostle Paul to have written of Jews and Gentiles in just the way in which chapter ii of this Epistle is written. He saw them from the position of one who had been a strict Jew, and had looked at Gentiles across 'the middle wall of partition' (ii. 14), and who had then been converted to Christ and become the apostle to the Gentiles.

A little more must be said about the teaching on the unity of the Church. It is argued that the concept of Ephesians is here more akin to that of Ignatius than to the position with which we are familiar from Paul's Epistles, where it is usually only the unity of the local church that is considered. It is said that this Epistle must date from the time when sects began to appear and abound. It is true that the author in Ephesians develops concepts of the nature and function of the Church that are in advance of anything in other Pauline letters (e.g. in ii. 20–22, iii. 10, 21, v. 23–32), but in the other Epistles we do find a view of the Church universal, not just the local church, and indeed a regard for the functions of the Church reaching beyond this world (e.g. see 1 Cor. iv. 9, xii. 28, xv. 9; Gal. i. 13; Phil. iii. 6). We should expect development and increasing understanding in a man with as virile and receptive a mind as Paul's; and if he had just been dealing with the cosmic significance of Christ in Colossians, it is not surprising that he should go on to deal in another letter with the cosmic place of the Church. Then there is a great difference between the thought of Ephesians and that of the Ignatian letters in the matter of Church unity. In the former the whole emphasis is on spiritual unity without reference to organization, while in the latter it is on unity under a single leader, the bishop.

One other particular argument should be considered at this point. It is asked: Would an apostle speak as the writer of this Epistle does in ii. 20 and iii. 5 of 'holy apostles and prophets' as those to whom the message is revealed, and as the foundation of the Church? Mitton (p. 19) says that the emphasis on their authority 'is reminiscent of the campaign for the proper recognition of duly authorized leaders which took place in the generation after Paul'. Yet in 1 Corinthians iii. 10 and ix. 2 Paul spoke of the apostles as the first builders on the foundation of Jesus Christ and such building work was the sign and seal of the genuineness of an apostle. Paul realized the priority of the position of the apostles (1 Cor. xii. 28), and without pride he felt the dignity and responsibility of his own place amongst them (1 Cor. ix. 1; Gal. i. 11–17, ii. 6–9); and certainly in Ephesians there is no undue stress on apostolic authority. It hardly needs to be added that the New Testament use of the word 'holy' did not involve the connotation of special sanctity of life, but rather the emphasis on the calling to dedication of life (see on i. 1).

There are in fact, on the other hand, even more cogent arguments for placing this Epistle not long, if at all, after the lifetime of Paul. It was in use very early. Probably Clement of Rome in the year 95 knew it. Hippolytus says that Basilides, the Ophites and the Valentinians used it, and they are among the earliest of Gnostic sects. The second-century evidence of the use of the Epistle is something which those who doubt its Pauline authorship find difficult to explain. Then there is no reference in it to the persecution of Christianity, which would be strange indeed if it was first written for the churches of the Roman province of Asia about the time when the Apocalypse was written, or even somewhat earlier. There is, moreover, no reference to the heresies which became widespread in Asia not so very long after the death of Paul. These things, at least, point inevitably to the conclusion that if Ephesians was not written by Paul it must have been written not long after his death.

We must now turn to considerations that help us more directly to determine whether the Epistle itself is such as would have been more likely to come from the apostle than from another writing in his name.

VI. OTHER EVIDENCE FOR AUTHORSHIP

We noted at the very beginning of this Introduction that Ephesians is different in form from any other letter that we regard as Paul's. It is said with a real measure of truth that it is hardly a letter, but more a written sermon or homily. It is asked whether even a 'circular letter' written for a number of churches, as is Galatians, would have been written as impersonally as this is. It is also argued further, that such personal references as there are do not ring true. Would Paul have said to any Christians to whom he wrote, 'If ye have heard of the dispensation of the grace of God which is given me' (iii. 2)? In our comment on that verse below we shall show that this translation is not quite true to the original; there is an element of doubt such as Paul could hardly have expressed to the Ephesian church, but he might well call his readers to recognize and accept the fact that God has enlightened him with His wisdom. It is not unthinkable that Paul should speak in this way, and then say, 'when ye read, ye may perceive my knowledge in the mystery of Christ' (see iii. 4), especially if he realized that he was writing to Christians over a wide area, some of whom would know him well, but others little more than his name and apostleship.

Then iii. 8 raises a difficulty for some, when Paul speaks of himself as 'less than the least of all saints'. The words have been spoken of as an exaggerated imitation of 1 Corinthians xv. 8f., 'a mild and passionless echo of the amazed sense of personal unworthiness of grace which is expressed in the Corinthian verses' (Allan). Others find in these words one of the clearest marks of the Epistle's genuineness. Abbott comments that the expression does not derive from 'calculated imitation; it has the stamp of a spontaneous outflow of an intense feeling of unworthiness'. Bruce says, 'No disciple of Paul's would have dreamed of giving the apostle so low a place.' At least it is difficult to think of an imitator at one moment trying to show the greatness of Paul's understanding and statement of the gospel, as is Mitton's view of iii. 2–4, and the next moment giving him such a humble place.

That there is a difference in style between this and other Pauline letters is undoubted. The style here is more diffuse. There is no closely worked out argument. The doctrinal passages are lyrical rather than argumentative. There are long sentences, full of participles, synonymous expressions, epexegetic genitives (e.g. i. 3–14, 15–23, ii. 1–9, iii. 1–7). Yet if we have to compare the style with that of Colossians, we would not deem that of Colossians greater and more worthy, nor would we say that the difference is such as to make identity of authorship impossible. Differences could surely be explained on the basis of the difference of purpose between the two letters, and the inevitable difference between writing an epistle to meet a particular need and the attempt to set down on paper the result of a deep and fruitful meditation on the central themes of the gospel. In Ephesians there was no need for argument to meet objections and difficulties; we have rather what Dodd calls 'a prophetic declaration of incontrovertible, patent facts, in a new and lofty setting of eternal principles'.[1] The writer here 'does not argue, he makes dogmatic statements' (Lock); so he has scope for waxing lyrical. We may add that when Colossians (as in i. 12–22) and Romans (as in i. 1–6 and viii. 32–39) do the same, their style approaches most nearly to that of Ephesians.

Analysis of the vocabulary of Ephesians reveals that the Epistle has forty-two words not used elsewhere in the New Testament. This figure is not great when compared with those

[1] C. H. Dodd, *Ephesians, Colossians and Philemon* (Abingdon Commentary), 1929.

34

for other Pauline Epistles;[1] it would seem more significant that thirty-eight words are used elsewhere in the New Testament but not in other Pauline letters. But such arguments from vocabulary are precarious. It is necessary to study the subject-matter of the passages in which the words are found. For example, in Ephesians quite a number of the *hapax legomena* belong to such particular descriptions as that of the Christian armour. Some of the words listed as found in the New Testament but not elsewhere in Paul are not really peculiar to this Epistle, in that words with the same stem are found in others. Some, again, are common words that Paul or any other first-century writer might well have used.

Particular words merit special consideration, but this cannot be done fully here. A few examples may be taken. It is noted that *diabolos* is used only here and in the Pastorals, while the other Pauline letters use *Satanas*. Acts and John use the two indifferently, however, and there seems no reason why Paul should not have used *diabolos*. There are phrases such as 'in the heavenly places', 'the Father of glory', 'before the foundation of the world', which are said to be non-Pauline. Others mention as words that are not Pauline, *kosmokratōr* of vi. 12 ('ruler of this world'), *sōtērion* for 'salvation', *methodeia* for the 'wiles' of the devil. But we should not be surprised to find in such an Epistle as this, if Paul's, words not found in other Epistles, words more familiar to us from other strands of early Christian thought. The apostle's mind was fertile and open to influence from the phraseology of his opponents and so surely from the terminology of other Christians. More important is the argument which we have considered already, that certain key words like *mustērion* and *oikonomia* are used in Ephesians in a way that is different from their use in other Pauline Epistles. But in this case, as with vocabulary generally, an imitator would try to follow closely the Pauline usage, and the differences are as hard or harder to explain on the theory that another wrote Ephesians in the name of the apostle.

We have considered the special development of doctrine that we find in Ephesians, and we have compared the teaching

[1] For details of this comparison see Abbott, p. xv.

35

of the Epistle with that of Colossians. There are certain other arguments that have been used in the attempt to show that the Epistle includes doctrine and subject-matter that could hardly have come from the pen of the apostle. It is urged that in Ephesians a number of divine acts are ascribed to Christ that in other Epistles are ascribed to the Father—e.g. the work of reconciliation (ii. 16; cf. Col. i. 20, ii. 13f.); the appointment of apostles, prophets, etc. (iv. 11; cf. 1 Cor. xii. 28). But there are examples of the reverse proceeding. In iv. 32 (RV) it is said that 'God . . . in Christ forgave you' (cf. Col. iii. 13). Both ways of speaking of the works of God can be found in a number of Pauline Epistles. To the apostle, what is the work of the Father is the work of the Son. Since he could say, 'To us there is but one God, the Father, of whom are all things, and we in him; and one Lord Jesus Christ, by whom are all things, and we by him' (1 Cor. viii. 6), there can be no validity in this kind of argument. What God does, He does through Christ (2 Cor. v. 18f.); and what Christ does, He does according to the will of the Father.

To some, a more important argument is that the eschatology of Ephesians is realized rather than futurist as it is in Paul's earlier Epistles, and even in Philippians. It is sometimes said that ii. 7 and iii. 21 imply a long time before the end, as the writer of Ephesians envisages it. In the commentary we must consider whether this is a true interpretation of the actual passages. The eschatology of Colossians and Ephesians is certainly not unlike. That there is a change of emphasis from Paul's earlier Epistles is undoubted; but the hope of the parousia is not lost. The Holy Spirit is the earnest of the future inheritance, for the experience of salvation is not yet complete in the Christian's life here and now (i. 13f., iv. 30). The Church will one day in the future be presented spotless to Christ (v. 27). There will be a future day of reckoning when all will have to stand before God as Judge (v. 6, vi. 8). If a strong case could be made for there being a real difference between the eschatology of Colossians and Ephesians, that might have bearing on the question of authorship, but such a case cannot be made.

We have considered the way in which this Epistle deals with the matter of the relationship between Jews and Gentiles. Independently of this issue it is said that the Jews are treated in Ephesians in a way that Paul himself could never have treated them. In ii. 3 they are said to be guilty of the same immoralities as the Gentiles, while in ii. 11f. there is what has been called a scornful reference to circumcision. It may be asked, however, whether Paul says less about the sins of the Jews, even sins of the flesh, in Romans ii. 21ff., and whether he speaks there any less severely than this Epistle does. Moreover, nothing more derogatory to circumcision is said in Ephesians than in Romans ii. 25ff., Philippians iii. 1f., and Colossians ii. 11; in fact the spirit of the four passages is very similar. (See further on ii. 11f.)

VII.   THE WORK OF AN IMITATOR OR OF THE APOSTLE?

We must say, with Mitton, that no single argument for or against Pauline authorship of Ephesians can be described as conclusive. It is the cumulative strength of all the arguments that must be considered. However, the earliest writers who cast doubt on the authenticity of the Epistle were content with negative arguments. More recently an attempt has been made, notably by Goodspeed[1] and Mitton, to suggest a situation after the time of Paul's death for which they believe that this Epistle was written.

Goodspeed's theory is that some years after the time of their being written, Paul's letters, written mostly to individual churches, were largely neglected or forgotten. A few people valued and kept them, and there were some who specially reverenced him for his letter to the church at Colossae, perhaps members of that church who were at first acquainted with that letter only. One man in particular knew and loved this letter. After Acts was published—Goodspeed puts that at about the year 85—and Paul was seen to stand out in all his greatness for his apostolic labours, this man decided to find as many as he could of Paul's letters. He collected them, read

[1] E. J. Goodspeed, *The Meaning of Ephesians*, 1933.

and re-read them, filled his mind with them, but most of all with Colossians which he knew first and loved most. Then he decided to republish them with an introduction that would lift the message of Paul above the topical issues of other days and would be simply a restatement of his understanding of the eternal truth of God in Christ. He did not want to obtrude his own personality, and so he wrote in Paul's name, and longed that the message of Paul might be heard again through him. Goodspeed says that this fact accounts for Ephesians being a 'mosaic of Pauline materials', 'almost a Pauline anthology'. The close similarity to Colossians is thus accounted for; the difficulties that have been felt about Pauline authorship are resolved. Goodspeed even goes so far as to guess that Onesimus was the author. His views have won much support, especially in America.

The English scholar Mitton has adopted the essentials of Goodspeed's theory, and believes that the relationship of Ephesians to the other Pauline Epistles and to Colossians in particular is to be explained in some such way as this. The dependence was thus not a literary dependence; the writing was done by one whose mind was filled with Paul's Epistles. Only at the end, in the reference to Tychicus, did he refer to his copy.

There are several main difficulties in the way of accepting such a theory. The first is the strong external evidence of Pauline authorship, and the very early use of the Epistle which we have noted above. It is in fact one of the Pauline Epistles best attested in the second-century Christian writings, and there is never any doubt expressed about its authenticity. Then there are features that are so typically Pauline that we would hardly expect to find them in an imitator. There is the characteristically Pauline way of connecting together doctrinal truth and moral duty. There is the Pauline habit of breaking off at a word to deal with a new subject (iii. 1–14; cf. Rom. v. 13ff.; Phil. iii. 1ff.). We cannot ultimately argue from the similarity or the differences in vocabulary and phraseology—as we have seen, the argument can be taken either way. But in this Epistle we have the unrestrained praise of the glory of

Christ, the uninhibited declaration of the wonder of His purpose for His Church, not in the measured terms of one who writes under a sense of obligation to follow faithfully his great predecessor, but under the free inspiration of the Spirit.

However differently pseudonymity may have been regarded in the ancient world from the way that we would regard it, we find in this Epistle such a combination of authority and humility, and such an expression of privilege and responsibility (both Pauline traits), as would be very hard to imitate effectively. Any imitator is betrayed by his inferiority, but, as Scott says, this Epistle 'contains nothing which might not have been written by Paul, while it is everywhere marked by a grandeur and originality of thought which seem utterly beyond the reach of any mere imitator'. Could an imitator have produced a work so like those of the apostle, and yet written with such freedom and originality, showing such a profound advance on Paul's thought in Colossians? An even more relevant question is, Would a person of such spiritual genius have followed Colossians so closely? The explanations of Goodspeed and Mitton are not adequate. It is possible, though unlikely, that there was a person of such spiritual calibre—otherwise unknown to us—in the generation after Paul's death, as could write like this. Yet the fact remains that the greatness of such an author and his dependence on Colossians (and other Pauline writings) are hard to put together. As Dodd puts it, 'Do we find such faithful dependence and such daring originality in one and the same person?'[1]

That there is point in many of the difficulties that have been raised concerning the authenticity of Ephesians cannot be denied. The special features of the Epistle when set alongside other Pauline letters demand explanation. But we would still ask whether the difficulties are lessened at all by positing an imitator. It seems that by far the most likely solution is still the traditional one. We suppose therefore that Paul wrote Colossians from his confinement in Rome to meet special difficulties and dangers in the church at Colossae. Then, as he

[1] C. H. Dodd, *Ephesians, Colossians and Philemon* (Abingdon Commentary), 1929.

thought over and expressed the truth of the Person of Christ, he was led on in his meditation to dwell on God's purpose in Christ as it is to be worked out in the Church. He thought not just of Colossae, but of all the churches, especially those of the Roman province of Asia. He saw how they needed to be given a vision of the greatness of their calling, and of the importance of the life and unity of the Church as the Body of Christ. So, shortly after writing Colossians, he wrote Ephesians. Colossians iv. 15f. refers to a letter not written to Laodicea, but which would reach Colossae from Laodicea. In other words, it seems that this letter, which he speaks of as written at the same time as Colossians, was in the nature of a circular letter. We believe that it is very probable, therefore, that the Epistle before us is the one to which Colossians iv. 15f. refers. The likelihood is increased if we consider that as the church of Colossae saw fit to preserve the little letter to Philemon, they would surely be anxious to preserve this general letter sent to the churches of the area.

Thus we imagine Colossians written, then Ephesians. Then the apostle penned the conclusion to Colossians, and immediately turned from writing that to address his closing personal message to the wider group of churches: 'that ye also may know my affairs . . . Tychicus . . . shall make known to you all things.' So Tychicus went off as bearer of the two letters and also of the personal letter to Philemon. He would have received explicit instructions concerning the churches of Asia to which he should take it. No one name was put in the address of our Epistle; the messenger could put in the relevant name at each place. In the years that followed several of the churches might have been found in possession of a copy. Perhaps only that in Ephesus had a name in it, and as Ephesus was the most famous church the letter would be copied most frequently from there, and so came to be named as we have it, 'The Epistle of Paul the Apostle to the Ephesians'.

ANALYSIS

I. INTRODUCTION (i. 1–23).

    a. Salutation (i. 1, 2).
    b. Praise for God's purpose and blessings in Christ (i. 3-14).
    c. Prayer for divine enlightenment (i. 15-23).

II. LIFE IN CHRIST (ii. 1–iii. 21).

    a. New life from the dead (ii. 1-10).
    b. The reconciliation of Jews and Gentiles (ii. 11-22).
    c. The privilege of proclamation (iii. 1-13).
    d. Renewed prayer (iii. 14-21).

III. UNITY IN THE BODY OF CHRIST (iv. 1–16).

    a. Maintaining the unity (iv. 1-6).
    b. Diversity in unity (iv. 7-16).

IV. PERSONAL STANDARDS (iv. 17–v. 21).

    a. New life to replace the old (iv. 17-24).
    b. Truth and love to replace falsehood and bitterness (iv. 25-v. 2).
    c. Light to replace darkness (v. 3-14).
    d. Wisdom to replace folly (v. 15-21).

V. RELATIONSHIPS (v. 22–vi. 9).

    a. Husbands and wives (v. 22-33).
    b. Children and parents (vi. 1-4).
    c. Servants and masters (vi. 5-9).

VI. CONCLUSION (vi. 10–24).

    a. The Christian conflict (vi. 10-20).
    b. Final message and greeting (vi. 21-24).

COMMENTARY

I. INTRODUCTION (i. 1-23)

a. Salutation (i. 1, 2)

1. All Paul's letters begin in a similar way. Following the style of the letter-writing of the day, he mentions first the writer, then the readers, and then comes the greeting. But the conventional manner of the time is lifted to a higher level. Writer and readers are described from the standpoint of their relationship to God in Christ; and the conventional greeting has become a Christian benediction.

Apostle is the title Paul most frequently gives himself. It speaks of the great privilege, but also of the divine compulsion, of the commission laid upon him. He could not think of himself in his relationship to men except in terms of his being sent to all with the gospel (cf. 2 Cor. v. 16). He is what he is *by the will of God*; and this is no mere permission, as the use of the same word in verses 5, 9 and 11 makes clear. It is God's positive purpose that makes Paul a man under authority, and enables him to write with authority. He is always at pains to stress that his calling is due to no personal merit (cf. 1 Cor. xv. 9; Gal. i. 13-15; 1 Tim. i. 12-16); his authority is not self-assumed. Both are entirely of God (cf. especially Gal. i. 1); and on that fact he relies, especially when his mission is challenged.

The frequent New Testament designation of Christians as *saints* is the first of a number of words in chapter i whose meaning can be understood fully only by a consideration of their Old Testament background. The saints are the holy ones, *hagioi*. In Old Testament days the tabernacle, the temple, the sabbath, and the people themselves were holy as they were consecrated, or set apart, for the service of God. A person is not a 'saint' in this sense by personal merit; he is one set apart by God, and in consequence he is called to live in holiness. Thus the word expresses at once the privilege and the responsibility of the calling of every Christian, not the attainment of a select few. As we have seen in the Introduction when considering the destination of the Epistle, the words *at Ephesus* are absent from some of the best MSS, and yet grammar almost certainly requires a place-name in the original. So we have concluded that it is likely that Ephesus was only one of a number of places to which this letter was sent.

The faithful (pistoi), a term often used for Christians in the New Testament, may mean those who have faith, or those who show fidelity. Here both ideas may be included; they are believers and their calling is to faithfulness. Nor is the meaning simply that the people addressed have faith in the Lord. The phrase *in Christ Jesus*, so frequently used by Paul, especially in this Epistle, sums up very much of his understanding of the gospel. It, or an equivalent, is used eleven times in verses 1–14 alone. Christians not only have faith in Him; their life is in Him. As the root in the soil, the branch in the vine (cf. Jn. xv. 1ff.), the fish in the sea, the bird in the air, so the place of the Christian's life is in Christ. Physically his life is in the world; spiritually it is lifted above the world to be in Christ (cf. Col. iii. 1–3). We have a pointed juxtaposition of two phrases as Paul addresses his readers in Colossians i. 2 as 'in Christ' and 'in Colossae'. There is the implication that wherever the Christian may be, in whatever difficult environment, threatened by materialism or paganism, in danger of being engulfed by the power of the state or overwhelmed by the pressures of non-Christian life, he is *in Christ*. This is not mysticism, but is intended to express the very practical truth that the Christian, if faithful to his calling, will not try to be self-sufficient, or to move beyond the limits of the purpose and control and love of Christ, nor will he turn to the world for guidance, inspiration and strength. He finds all his satisfaction and his every need met in Him, and not in any other place nor from any other source. This description of the Christian's life is implied in the expression being 'baptized into Jesus Christ' (Rom. vi. 3), as baptism is the outward sign of entrance into such a life. It also involves the truth that the Christian's corporate existence is in the Body of Christ which is His Church.

2. The common Greek greeting was *chairein* (see Acts xv. 23, xxiii. 26; Jas. i. 1); here Paul uses the cognate word *charis* (*grace*). *Peace* was the common Hebrew greeting (*shalōm*). It was used, for example, when the seventy were sent out by the Lord (Lk. x. 5). As in all his greetings, Paul brings grace and peace together, and the two may be said to sum up all the gifts of Christ. The greeting has thus become a blessing, or a prayer that his readers may know fully the free, undeserved favour of God, restoring them to Himself, and adding to them all that they need (see further on iii. 2 for *charis*); and that they may know peace with God, peace in their hearts, and peace with one another. The two words are in fact twin themes of the Epistle, as of the gospel of Christ itself. The grace and peace come *from God our Father*, as the Source of all things, *and from the Lord Jesus Christ*, who by what He has done has brought them to men.

b. Praise for God's purpose and blessings in Christ (i. 3–14)

3. Now, after his brief greeting, and before he expresses his thanks for the welfare of those to whom he is writing (verses 15, 16), the apostle goes straight into a great paean of praise— one long sentence, impossible to analyse, in which each successive thought crowds in on the one before. There is no predetermined order in the enumeration of the blessings; the contemplation of one leads naturally to the next—election from the very beginning; sonship by adoption; redemption, which means forgiveness; insight into God's all-embracing purpose; the privilege (both for Jews and Gentiles) of becoming His people; and the sealing of the Spirit, which is the earnest of the final inheritance. Three particular notes sound right through this great doxology. First, from eternity to eternity God works all things according to His perfect plan. All history, all men, all that exists in heaven and on earth are included in His purpose. Secondly, that purpose is fulfilled in Christ, and thus in Him every blessing that men have is found. Thirdly, as far as men are concerned, its goal is the very practical one, that they should be 'to the praise of (his) glory'.

In the New Testament the word *blessed* (*eulogētos*) is used only of God. He alone is worthy to be blessed. Men are blessed when they receive His blessings; God is blessed when He is praised for all that He freely bestows on man and on His world. Above all He is blessed as *the God and Father of our Lord Jesus Christ* (cf. Rom. xv. 6; 1 Pet. i. 3; Rev. i. 6); for He is revealed to us supremely in Christ who, as Son, is the perfect image of the Father (see Jn. i. 18 and Heb. i. 1–3).

The Greek translated *who hath blessed* is an aorist participle, which may refer to a particular occasion in the past when those blessings were first received, or when He brought them to men; but the tense is not of necessity to be pressed. Strictly also the noun is singular; RV 'with every spiritual blessing' is therefore more accurate. From Him comes one continuous flow of blessing, and this is to be conceived not chiefly in terms of the material gifts of which we think most readily, but in terms of the spiritual that transcend but include the material, for the true appreciation of the things we see is dependent on our enjoyment of the things of the Spirit.

This is made clearer still by the defining phrase that follows, *in heavenly places*. The Greek, *en tois epouraniois*, means literally 'in the heavenly things', but the other uses of the phrase show that it is much more than a synonym for *spiritual*, and that our translators are justified in their rendering. In this Epistle, Christ is said to be exalted to be 'in the heavenly places' (i. 20); the wisdom of God is being made known to the principalities and powers 'in heavenly places' (iii. 10); the same phrase is used of the sphere of the spiritual conflict against the forces of evil (vi. 12); and, most closely connected with the subject here, in ii. 6 Christians are said to be 'raised up' and made to 'sit together in heavenly places in Christ Jesus'. Their life is lifted above the commonplace. It is in the world, but it is also in heaven, unlimited by the material things that pass away (cf. Phil. iii. 20, RV). Life now, if it is life *in Christ*, is in the heavenly realm.

4. The purpose of God is shown to be not of this earth but of heaven by the fact that it existed *before the foundation of the world*. Election, as Calvin said, is 'the foundation and first cause' of all blessings. And the doctrine of election runs through the whole Bible. Israel was chosen, not for any merit, but to be the means of the fulfilling of the eternal purpose of God (see Dt. vii. 6–8; Is. xlii. 1, xliii. 20f.). In the New Testament the principle of election is confirmed, but there is no longer a national limitation—a truth that this Epistle later develops and expounds. This doctrine of election, or predestination, is not raised as a subject of controversy or speculation. It is not set in opposition to the self-evident fact of the free will of man. It involves a paradox that the New Testament does not seek to resolve, and that our finite minds cannot fathom. Paul emphasizes both the sovereign purpose of God and man's free will. He took the gospel of grace and offered it to all. Then to those who had accepted the gospel he set forward the doctrine of election for two reasons, both of which we find linked similarly together in John xv. 16, Romans viii. 29, 2 Thessalonians ii. 13, 2 Timothy i. 9 and 1 Peter i. 2. First, the Christian needs to realize that his faith rests completely on the work of God and not on the unsteady foundation of anything in himself. It is all the Lord's work, and in accordance with His plan, a plan that reaches back *before the foundation of the world*. Second, God has chosen us *that we should be holy and without blame before him* (cf. v. 27 and Col. i. 22). Election is not simply to salvation, but to holiness of life. We were 'created in Christ Jesus', ii. 10 is to express it, 'unto good works, which God hath before ordained that we should walk in them'. We were 'foreordained to be conformed to the image of his Son' (Rom. viii. 29, RV).

The ideal and goal of the Christian life, therefore, is perfect holiness (cf. Mt. v. 48), expressed in its positive aspect as dedication of life (see on verse 1), and negatively as freedom from every fault. Behind the word *amōmous*, used similarly in

Philippians ii. 15, and here translated *without blame* (RV, 'without blemish') lies a use in connection with Old Testament sacrifices. Only a perfect animal could be offered to God (e.g. see Lv. i. 3, 10). So, as Hebrews ix. 14 puts it, Christ offered Himself morally and spiritually 'without blemish' to God (RV; cf. 1 Pet. i. 19). The life of the Christian is also to be 'without blemish', not merely by human standards but *before him* who is the Witness of all that a man does, and thinks, and says. (For this same emphasis of the apostle on man's life lived every moment in the sight of God see Rom. i. 9; 2 Cor. iv. 2; Gal. i. 20; 1 Thes. ii. 5.)

The words *in love* may be taken either with what follows or with what precedes, and the differing opinions of translators and commentators ancient and modern indicate that it is not possible to be dogmatic regarding the intention of the writer. RSV translates 'he destined us in love to be his sons'. This may be right; at least it is a truth that this whole section emphasizes. But the position of the phrase, and its use elsewhere in the Epistle for man's love rather than God's love (iii. 17, iv. 2, 16, v. 2), make the rendering accepted by the AV, RV and NEB more likely. The point, then, is that holiness of life is only made perfect in and through love (cf. 1 Thes. iii. 12f.).

5. For *predestinated* RV has 'foreordained'; the Greek *proorisas* means literally 'marked out beforehand'. It is simply another word that expresses the fact that God's plan for His people is from eternity. That plan is *the adoption of children by Jesus Christ to himself.* Men were created for life in fellowship with God, as sons with the Father (Gn. i. 26; Acts xvii. 28). By sin that privilege was forfeited, but by grace, in and through Christ, restoration to sonship is made possible (Jn. i. 12). *Adoption*—a Roman and not a Jewish practice—is the best way to describe this (cf. Rom. viii. 15, 23; Gal. iv. 5), because an adopted son has his position by grace and not by right, and yet is brought into the family on the same footing as a son by birth.

What God has done was *according to the good pleasure of his will.* Both expressions here speak of His purpose and sovereign

47

love. *Good pleasure (eudokia)* has two meanings in Scripture. It is sometimes the goodwill felt towards a person (cf. Lk. ii. 14); but where there is no reference to a person who feels this goodwill, it normally means 'purpose', as fits the context here and in verse 9 (cf. Mt. xi. 26)—though there may be a suggestion of the first meaning as well (cf. the use of the corresponding verb in Lk. xii. 32). It is the purpose of His desiring *(thelēmatos)*, what Moule describes as His 'deliberate, beneficent resolve' *(CB)*.

6. In this verse we have the first occurrence of the phrase *to the praise of the glory of his grace* which comes three times in this section, like a refrain at the end of successive stanzas of a poem. God's glory is the showing forth of His very nature, and grace is His supreme self-manifestation. (See Ex. xxxiii. 18f., xxxiv. 5–7.) As Israel was chosen to live to His praise (Is. xliii. 21), so those who in Christ are received as sons must show forth the Father's nature of grace and thus glorify Him (cf. v. 1; Mt. v. 45; Lk. vi. 35). The word *grace* is too full of meaning for Paul to pass over lightly (cf. verse 7 and ii. 7). It must be qualified. The Greek verb *charitoō*, used in the clause *wherein he hath made us accepted in the beloved*, is from the noun *charis (grace)*. (Compare the constructions in verses 19, 20, ii. 4 and iv. 1.) Sometimes it has been taken to mean 'the grace with which He has made us gracious'; so Chrysostom (quoted by Abbott) says, 'it is as if one were to take a leper and change him into a lovely youth'. But it is more in accord with the context to take it as 'the favour with which He has favoured us', or as the 'grace, which he freely bestowed on us' (so RV). It is the objective grace of God which is in mind, God's undeserved favour towards us, rather than any virtue that we derive.

This, it is emphasized again, is *in* Christ who is *the beloved*. This description was used as a name for Israel, and so came to be used as a title of Israel's greatest Representative, the Messiah.[1] But its literal meaning is not lost (cf. Mt. iii. 17 and xvii. 5) as the parallel expression in Colossians i. 13—'the

[1] See Robinson, pp. 229ff.

Son of his love' (rv)—indicates. As Dale puts it, 'Christ dwells for ever in the infinite love of God, and as we are in Christ, the love of God for Christ is in a wonderful manner ours.'

7. The blessing of *redemption* follows, for man's prior need of grace is of redeeming, restoring grace. Such redemption is found *in* Christ—not merely through Him, but by men coming to live in Him (cf. Rom. iii. 24; Col. i. 14). Again the Old Testament provides the background for our understanding. There, provision was made for the redemption of lands or persons that had passed from their original owner to become the property of another (see Lv. xxv. 25-27, 47-49; Nu. xviii. 15). The people of Israel, moreover, were themselves essentially a redeemed people. They had been slaves in Egypt, and later, through their own sinfulness, in Babylon as well. Yet God had redeemed them, and by redemption they were made His people (Ex. xv. 13; Dt. vii. 8; Is. xlviii. 20, lii. 9). The fundamental idea of redemption is that of the setting free of a thing or a person that has come to belong to another. Sometimes, in both Old and New Testaments, there is no accompanying reference to the price paid for redemption, and the word has simply the primary sense of release (e.g. Lk. xxi. 28; Rom. viii. 23; Heb. ix. 15). But Paul's mind often dwelt on the thought of the costliness of redemption, and in a number of places in the New Testament this is obviously present (see Acts xx. 28; 1 Cor. vi. 20; 1 Pet. i. 18f.; Rev. v. 9).

We cannot say here that Paul speaks explicitly of the cost of redemption, but he says immediately that it is *through his blood*. Nor would he have hesitated to say that what is the means of liberation is in fact also the price. In the case of the Passover, a sacrifice was associated with the redemption of the people. The primary object of most of the old sacrifices, however, was the setting aside of sin. Instilled deeply into the consciousness of the people was the fact that sin could not be set aside lightly. Sin required sacrifice; 'without shedding of blood is no remission' (Heb. ix. 22; cf. Lv. xvii. 11). Christ fulfilled the need expressed throughout the Old Testament sacrificial system. His death means that *blood* has been shed as a sacrifice for sin; it may also be described in terms of sin's defeat and so the release of man from its bondage. The sacrifice is thus the means of redemption which is *the forgiveness of sins*. Sin involves the bondage of mind and will and members, but forgiveness is freedom, and *aphesis*, the word used here, means literally the loosing of a person from that which binds him. This forgiveness, Paul says, is *according to the riches of his grace*, grace which is rich beyond man's understanding and infinitely beyond any earthly wealth (cf. Mt. vi. 19f.; 1 Tim. vi. 17ff.; Heb. xi. 26). Six times in this letter the apostle speaks thus of the riches of God, revealed and made available to men, the wealth of His grace and mercy and glory (verse 18, ii. 4, 7, iii. 8, 16), and the expression is characteristically Pauline (cf. Rom. ii. 4, ix. 23, xi. 33; 2 Cor. viii. 9; Col. i. 27, ii. 2). And God's giving is not merely out of those *riches* but *according to* their measure (cf. Phil. iv. 19).

8. Not yet, however, are the epithets of grace exhausted. 'Abound' is another favourite Pauline word, expressive of the superabundance of God's giving, the overflow as of a fountain from a deep and abundant source; and also, by His grace, expressive of the quality expected in a Christian's life (1 Thes. iii. 12, iv. 1, 10). Then in the words *in all wisdom and prudence* we have the fourth of the great blessings which the apostle enumerates. God not only receives and forgives. Those whom He has reconciled to Himself as sons He also enlightens with the understanding of His purpose. This is developed further in chapters ii and iii. In many classical writers a distinction is made between *wisdom* (*sophia*) and *prudence* (*phronēsis*). It is not always maintained, but probably it is right in this passage to distinguish *wisdom*, which Robinson defines as 'the knowledge which sees into the heart of things, which knows them as they really are', from *prudence* which he calls 'the understanding which leads to right action'. If this is correct, it follows that the wisdom of God is not merely intellectual or academic, a higher philosophy such as that which the Gnostics in the early days of the Church boasted that they possessed; it is also the source of understanding in the details of daily living (cf.

Phil. i. 9f.). As Barclay puts it, 'Christ gives to men the ability to see the great ultimate truths of eternity and to solve the problems of each moment of time.'

9. Men have such wisdom and prudence because God reveals His *will* concerning the goal and purpose of life, and concerning its details (cf. Col. i. 9). What He makes known the apostle calls the *mystery*. In classical Greek the word *mustērion* had two meanings. The root meaning was that into which one was initiated, and from this it came to mean also a secret of any kind. In the LXX it is used of what is revealed by God (e.g. Dn. ii. 19), and also of the secret that a tale-bearer tells (e.g. Ecclus. xxii. 22). Thus its Christian use is not of necessity derived from its use in the heathen mystery cults so common in New Testament days. Paul could not have failed, however, to think of this use, and no doubt he consciously compared with the strange and baseless heathen mysteries the truth of God in Christ revealed to all who will receive it, and given to His Church to proclaim to the world. For Paul, the essential mystery was the way in which God through Christ brings men back into fellowship with Himself. More than that, it is the way in which He brings into a restored unity the whole universe that has been disordered by man's rebellion and sin. Thus the word in the New Testament conveys the thought not of something mysterious, but something revealed, and regularly words expressive of disclosure rather than keeping secret go with *mustērion* (cf. Col. i. 26, ii. 2, iv. 3). Nevertheless the word does bear the significance of truth not previously known but now revealed (Rom. xvi. 25), and the even more important fact that understanding depends on God's will to reveal, and on man's desire to receive insight that must be God-given.[1]

Then in the end of this verse we see that, just as in verses 7 and 8 the apostle sought to describe and extol in so many ways the munificence of God's grace, here he wants to express the wonder of His purpose. He does so by using three synonyms (two of them have been used already in verse 5), thus describing

---

[1] For a careful study of the word see Robinson, pp. 234ff.

the *mystery* as *his will*, *his good pleasure*, and that which God has *purposed in himself* (or 'in Christ', if *autō* is read rather than *hautō*. So NEB).

10. In this sovereign plan what God has done and is doing in Christ is spoken of as being with a view to the *dispensation* belonging to *the fulness of times*—'to be put into effect when the time was ripe' (NEB). Simpson aptly renders it the divine 'programme of history'. We must, however, study the word *dispensation* to see more clearly the apostle's meaning. The word here (*oikonomia*) is one that was used either for the administration of a household (*oikos*), or for the responsibility of the one who administered it. It is used several times in the New Testament in this latter sense of stewardship. For the Church is the household of God, Jesus Christ is Chief Steward, and under Him His ministers are called to serve as stewards (see 1 Cor. iv. 1f., ix. 17; Tit. i. 7; 1 Pet. iv. 10). Here it is the government or arrangement of things for God's people, and for the whole universe, that is in view. Jesus Christ orders everything in its full time, and in infinite wisdom orders the time of all things. It is also to be noted here that the word used for *times* is not *chronos* which connotes the passage of time in days and months and years, but *kairos* which speaks of particular times, the decisive times of fulfilment in the purposes of God. Bruce well paraphrases: 'When all the times and seasons which the Father has fixed by His own authority have run their course, God's age-long purpose which He planned in Christ will attain its full fruition.'

For the Greek word *anakephalaiōsasthai*, translated *gather together* by AV, RV has 'sum up' and RSV 'unite'. The word was used of gathering things together and presenting them as a whole. The Greek practice was to add up a column of figures and put the sum at the top, and this name was given to the process. So the word was used in rhetoric for summing up an address at the end, and thus showing the relation of each part to the complete argument. In Romans xiii. 9 it is used for the summing up of the commandments in the one demand of love. Three ideas are present in the word here—restoration, unity, and the headship of Christ. Weymouth brings out all three when he translates 'the purpose . . . of restoring the whole creation to find its one Head in Christ'. All things were created in Christ (Col. i. 16). Through sin endless disorder and distintegration have come into the world; but in the end all things will be restored to their intended function and to their unity by being brought back to the obedience of Christ (cf. Col. i. 20).

The phrase *all things*, which in Greek expresses absolute universality (cf. Col. i. 17; Heb. i. 3), is qualified by *both which are in heaven and which are on earth*. Paul has in view the whole creation, spiritual and material. At the time of writing he was concerned with a heresy in Asia Minor, which placed many spiritual powers in opposition to Christ, and others as mediators between God and man. His answer to such teaching —explicit in Colossians and only implicit in this Epistle—is that there is One alone who can and will reconcile and unify all things. It is a heresy of our times to divide life into sacred and secular. Christ is concerned in all things, and all will find their true place and unity in Him. This Epistle, moreover, does not merely speak of a distant goal, but presents the task of the Church now in a world divided by barriers of race, colour, culture and political system, as that of bringing all things and all men into the captivity of obedience to Christ (cf. 2 Cor. x. 5), and so back to find their true functions and unity in Him.

This verse has been used as the keystone of the doctrine of 'Universalism', that all men shall be saved in the end. It does imply that in the end everything and every being in existence will be under His authority, but it is dangerous to press a doctrine from a verse without regard for the balance of the evidence of Scripture as a whole, and, in this case, without respect for the solemn presentation from one end of Scripture to the other of the alternatives of life and death dependent on the acceptance or rejection of God's salvation.

11. The closing phrase of verse 10 reiterated that the blessing mentioned there, like the others, is received *in* Christ. The same applies to the next, for Paul continues *in whom also we* *have obtained an inheritance.* Basically the verb here, *klēroō*, means 'choose by lot'. Often in its use the idea of the 'lot' disappeared, and the thought is essentially that which recurs often in the Old Testament when Israel is spoken of as God's portion (see Dt. iv. 20, ix. 29; Zc. ii. 12). The word *inheritance* (*klēronomia*; see verse 14) is a cognate word, and it follows, though it is not exactly what is expressed here, that those who are God's portion have their inheritance in Him. At this point Paul is speaking of the Old Testament beginning of the out-working of God's purpose for men, as he says that *we*, the Jews, became His people.

The change of personal pronouns in this Epistle between first and second persons several times signifies the difference between Jews and Gentiles. The end of verse 12 will make clear that this is the case here. The divine plan for man's redemption began with the Jews *being predestinated according to the purpose of him who worketh all things after the counsel of his own will.* The same word *predestinated* has been used in verse 5. They were 'marked out beforehand' to have a part in His purpose. And that purpose is not, as it were, blueprints of history, which are followed out automatically as the years and cen-turies pass by. It is the purpose of the personal God who is active in the world, working out His own will in wisdom and grace (cf. Rom. viii. 28). Such is the force of the words used here: first, His 'in-working' (*energountos*) or 'energizing' all things; then His determined plan (*boulē*; cf. Acts ii. 23, iv. 28, xiii. 36, xx. 27); then His wish or will (*thelēma*; see on verses 5 and 9). Thus Weymouth translates, 'whose might carries out in everything the design of His own will'.

12. The goal of this His plan for the Jews, the apostle says, was that they should be *to the praise of his glory.* For no other purpose did God choose Abraham, and work out His design in the history of Israel, than that they should show forth in the world His glory (Is. xliii. 21), His revealed character and nature (see on verse 6). Here, then, Paul is speaking of those *who first trusted in Christ.* More correctly the verb means 'hoped' (RV), and it has the prefix *pro-* which may mean either that they hoped in Christ before others (but after the incarnation), or that they had set their hope on Christ before He came. The fact that the Jews had the knowledge of the gospel before the Gentiles is expressed in Romans i. 16, ii. 9f. It is more likely, however, that the reference here is to the Jewish hope in 'the Christ' (the Greek has the article) before He came (cf. Acts xxviii. 20). As Scott comments, 'Ages before Christ had appeared they had known that he was coming and had been looking forward to him. Their religion, in the last resort, had turned on the hope for Christ. . . .'

13. In the Greek there is no verb in the opening relative clause of this verse. AV may be right in repeating the verb that immediately precedes. Alternatively, we may go back to the verb of verse 11, 'you also have obtained an inheritance'; or we can look on to the verb that comes later in this verse, as does RV. Perhaps none of these is exactly what was intended and we may come closest to the meaning by supplying the verb 'to be'. 'You too', you Gentiles, '. . . became incorporate in Christ' (NEB). Gentiles without hope before (see ii. 12) have come into the same purpose as the Jews, and for the same reasons. For Paul goes on to say what that involves for them.

The Gentiles had come into the purpose of God, because they had come to know Jesus as the Christ; and this transforming knowledge is described in two ways. First, it is *the word of truth*, i.e. the word that brought them the knowledge of ultimate reality, the revelation of God in His Son (cf. iv. 21; Col. i. 5). And secondly, that truth is *the gospel* or good news, because it is not only revelation, but also the message of the love and mercy and *salvation* of God for sinful men (cf. Rom. i. 16).

Hearing this word is vital, because by hearing alone comes the knowledge of the truth of the gospel (Rom. x. 14). But hearing is vain unless it leads to faith, the means by which alone, on man's side, God's blessings can be received. *Believed* is to be taken as having no predicate; *in whom* goes with what follows, for it is 'in Christ' that this new blessing comes, like every one of the others. Gentiles as well as Jews, having heard and believed, have been *sealed*. In the ancient world the seal was the personal sign of the owner or the sender of something important, and thus, as in a letter, it distinguished what was true from what was spurious. It also was the guarantee that the thing sealed had been carried intact. In New Testament times certain religious cults followed the practice of having their devotees tattooed with the emblem of the cult, and the initiates were then said to have been sealed. This may have been in Paul's mind here, and in the very different context of Galatians vi. 17, but not necessarily so. The Jews thought of circumcision as a seal (see Rom. iv. 11). The Holy Spirit is the Christian's seal. The experience of the Holy Spirit in his life is the final proof to him, and indeed a demonstration to others, of the genuineness of what he has believed, and provides the inward assurance that he belongs to God as a son (cf. Rom. viii. 15f.; Gal. iv. 6). Later on, perhaps because of the analogy of circumcision, perhaps because of the language used for initiation in the Mystery Cults, baptism came to be known as the seal of the Spirit. It is indeed 'an outward and visible sign' given to the Christian of the inward work of God. But here it is clearly intended that the Holy Spirit's presence is the seal. The Spirit in the believer's life is the undeniable mark of God's work in and for him. He is also the means by whom the Christian can be kept 'intact' till the day of the Lord. (It should be noticed that the contexts here and in iv. 30 and in 2 Cor. i. 21f., where the 'seal' is spoken of, all point forward to the full possession of God's blessings in the end.)

The Greek, taken by AV and RV as the *holy Spirit of promise*, can mean 'the promised holy Spirit' (NEB), the Spirit as promised in the Old Testament (e.g. Ezk. xxxvi. 26f., xxxvii. 1–14; Joel ii. 28f.), and then by the Lord (Lk. xxiv. 49; Jn. xiv–xvi; Acts i. 4f.). If this is the meaning it is a little strange that Paul did not simply use the participle. It seems more likely that he meant the Holy Spirit whose presence carries the promise of good things to come, for this is the thought that is developed in the metaphors of verse 14.

14. In a bargain between two parties *the earnest* (arrabōn—

a word that came into Greek from Phoenician traders) was the payment of part, which carried the assurance of full payment being made. The Greek word is used three times in the LXX of Genesis xxxviii. 17–20 for a pledge, and significantly the same word is used in modern Greek for an engagement ring (Bruce). The Christian's experience of the Spirit now is a foretaste and pledge of what will be his when he fully possesses his God-given inheritance. (Compare 2 Cor. i. 21f.— where it is also linked with the word 'seal'—2 Cor. v. 5, and also Rom. viii. 23 where, with a similar meaning, the Spirit is called 'the firstfruits'.)

Until the redemption of the purchased possession has sometimes been taken as meaning 'until the obtaining (in full) of our divine possession' (cf. Moffatt and RSV). In favour of this is the fact that it continues with the thought already expressed in the metaphor of the *earnest*. But the two words *redemption* (*apolutrōsis*) and *possession* (*peripoiēsis*), like many terms in this section, are technical terms that are interpreted most naturally in the light of their Old Testament use which Christians were making their own. The *redemption* is the setting free of the slaves of sin for them to become God's people. It has been so used in verse 7, and often in the New Testament has this meaning. Such redemption is said to be partly achieved now, but in the end will be achieved fully (see iv. 30; Rom. viii. 23; Lk. xxi. 28); God will then take completely from alien hands that which is His own. The object redeemed is God's own 'peculiar people', and this expression is used in 1 Peter ii. 9, calling to mind Exodus xix. 5 and perhaps Isaiah xliii. 21 and Malachi iii. 17.[1] Thus RV translates 'unto the redemption of God's own possession' and NEB 'when God has redeemed what is his own'. If we follow this, we must assume that 'the metaphor from a mercantile transaction has by this time been wholly dropped' (Robinson), and the Old Testament metaphors, more readily in the mind of an apostle, taken up again.

In either case this great doxology ends with the thought of the full possession of all that God has planned for men— Jews and Gentiles alike—and this, like all that has been given

[1] See Robinson, p. 148.

57

at each stage in the unfolding of God's purpose, is *unto the praise of his glory.*

c. Prayer for divine enlightenment (i. 15–23)

15. After the great doxology of verses 3–14 the apostle's mind turns to those to whom he is writing. He now gives thanks and prays for them, but this also is not simply in the conventional manner of contemporary letter-writing (see on verse 1 and Robinson, pp. 37f., 275ff.), but in the spirit of true Christian prayer. In particular—as the opening *wherefore* signifies—he prays in the light of the wealth of spiritual blessing of which he has just been writing. The thought of the purpose of God in Christ, the blessings of election, sonship, redemption, revelation, the gift of the Holy Spirit, leads naturally and inevitably to praise and prayer for the members of His Church (cf. iii. 14).

I also is rather 'I for my part'. Paul had *heard* of the fruit of the gospel among his readers, perhaps in the same way as he had heard of it in the church at Colossae (Col. i. 6-8). As we have seen,[1] the lack of more specific and detailed thanksgivings here, even such as Paul wrote to churches that he had never visited (Rom. i. 8; Col. i. 3–9), argues strongly against Ephesus (or Ephesus alone) being the original destination planned for this Epistle. At the same time the writer has definite readers in view, and can give thanks for their *faith in the Lord Jesus*, the basic thing that can lead to the experience of all that the same Lord Jesus seeks to do and to give. Nor is this *faith* a matter only of their personal relation to their Lord. It affects their conduct towards *all the saints*. AV, RSV and NEB have here the word *love* which is omitted by the RV following some ancient MSS. It is a little more likely that *love* was added to the original text (in agreement with Col. i. 4 and Phm. 5) than omitted by a copyist's slip, though its absence gives an expression without parallel in the New Testament. There is also a difficulty in using the same word *faith* in a different sense with the two objects that follow. The apostle may have

[1] See pp. 17ff.

spoken of their outgoing, undiscriminating *love unto all the saints,* and the word have dropped out from some MSS in error. Otherwise his meaning must be that their faith was evident, not only in their inward spiritual lives but in their relationships with all their fellow-Christians as well.

16. Two features of the apostle's prayer life are in evidence in this verse. We see in the first place its constancy. Paul exhorted others to 'pray without ceasing' (1 Thes. v. 17; cf. Eph. vi. 18; Rom. xii. 12; Col. iv. 2), and from all his letters we can form a clear impression of his earnest, unwearying prayer for 'all the churches' (see 2 Cor. xi. 28, and compare the introductions of almost all his letters). Secondly we see the place of thanksgiving in his prayer. He taught others that praise should be the unfailing accompaniment of intercession (Eph. v. 19f.; Phil. iv. 6; Col. iii. 15–17, iv. 2; 1 Thes. v. 18), and this also we see from his letters was a feature of his own praying. The phrase translated *making mention* could mean simply 'remembering' as RSV takes it, but it is probably more definite and specific than that.

17. He who hears and answers prayer is described firstly as *the God of our Lord Jesus Christ.* More frequently we have the title 'the God and Father of our Lord Jesus Christ' (see on verse 3), but here (where the following phrase doubtless has influenced the form of this) simply His *God,* that is, the God whom He acknowledges and whom He reveals to us. There is nothing in the expression which is contrary to His own sharing of the Godhead; for He could speak of the Father as 'my God' (Mt. xxvii. 46; Jn. xx. 17). Secondly, He is *the Father of glory.* (Compare the titles 'God of glory' in Acts vii. 2 and 'Lord of glory' in 1 Cor. ii. 8.) He is the Father to whom all glory belongs; for all the power and majesty revealed in creation, providence and redemption (see on verse 6) are His, and He the Source. Such a thought of who God is gives to prayer a sense of awe and strengthens faith in those who pray (cf. iii. 14f.).

The gift, above all others, which he asks from God for his

readers is *the spirit of wisdom and revelation* (cf. Col. i. 9). Sometimes in the Epistles the word *spirit* refers to the human spirit
(e.g. in iv. 23; Rom. i. 9; 2 Cor. vii. 13), or it may refer to a
quality of mind or soul that a man may receive or show, in
particular a spiritual attitude or endowment. So 1 Corinthians
iv. 21 and Galatians vi. 1 speak of 'the spirit of meekness' and
2 Corinthians iv. 13 of a 'spirit of faith'. Then often, of course,
it refers to the Holy Spirit of God. Robinson says, 'With the
article, very generally, the word indicates the personal Holy
Spirit; while without it, some special manifestation or bestowal
of the Holy Spirit is signified.' So probably here we should
take it as NEB 'the spiritual powers of wisdom and vision', and
understand these as possible only as the gift of the Spirit who
makes wise (see on verse 8), and who alone reveals the truth
(Jn. xiv. 26, xvi. 13; 1 Cor. ii. 12). Such wisdom and revelation,
moreover, come, not simply as the mind of man acquires
certain truths, nor even simply as such higher intelligence is
given from God, but by *the knowledge of him*, the personal
knowledge of God Himself, which in the Bible always connotes
the experience of life in union and fellowship with Him (see on
iv. 13). Paul put the prayer for wisdom first because to him the
gospel was so wonderful that it was impossible for men to see
the glory of it unless they were taught of God, and also
because he knew that the knowledge of God was life itself
(cf. Jn. xvii. 3; Phil. iii. 10).

18. Such knowledge of God is described further, as often in
both Old and New Testaments, as man's enlightenment. The
Old Testament gave men hope for the future in terms of the
coming of light into a world in darkness and as the opening of
the eyes of the blind (e.g. Is. ix. 2, xxxv. 5, xlii. 6, xlix. 6,
lx. 1f., 19). When Christ came His presence was described as
the dawning of a new day, the breaking in of the light of God
(Mt. iv. 16; Lk. i. 79; Jn. i. 9, viii. 12; 2 Cor. iv. 6). Apart from
Him, or in rejection of Him, the eyes of men's hearts are
closed, and they are in the darkness of sin and ignorance and
despair (Eph. v. 8; cf. Mt. xiii. 15; Rom. i. 21); but those who
receive Him into their lives find their *eyes . . . enlightened* and

made able to see (cf. Mt. xiii. 16f.; Acts xxvi. 18; Heb. vi. 4, x. 32). The AV *eyes of your understanding* more strictly should be 'the eyes of your heart' (RV; Gk. *kardias*) and we need to remember that in biblical expression the heart is not simply the seat of the emotions, nor the seat of the intellect or *understanding*, but the centre of the whole personality, 'the inner man in his entirety' (Barry). This is clear from the study of the use of the word in the Bible, but it is evident even here when we consider what the apostle now speaks of as the results or objects of this enlightenment of the heart.

The apostle prays that by the eyes of their heart being enlightened they *may know* three things. The first is *what is the hope of his calling*. The apostle can speak of 'your calling' (iv. 4), but in the desire to emphasize again that what they have depends on God's initiative, he speaks of it as *his calling*. This calling can be spoken of as having taken place in the past— God has called men to Himself (2 Tim. i. 9); or as continuing in the present (1 Thes. ii. 12, v. 24) and so involving a life-long vocation of service and sanctification (Eph. iv. 1; Phil. iii. 14; Heb. iii. 1). But also, because it is the call of the eternal God, it brings to men without hope (ii. 12) the expectation of an eternal destiny. This hope, moreover, is not just 'a vague and wistful longing for the triumph of goodness', but it is something assured because of the present possession of the Spirit as earnest (verse 14) and because of the faithfulness of the God who has promised the future inheritance.[1] The call of God, in other words, is effective not only in life now (cf. 1 Cor. xv. 19) but it gives the sure promise of life with Him as His sons for ever, and this hope in its turn should vitally affect life for the Christian in the here and now (1 Jn. iii. 2f.).

Secondly, he prays that they may know *what* are *the riches of the glory of his inheritance in the saints*. Some have taken this to mean what God possesses in His saints. They are 'the Lord's portion' as verse 11 has shown. But the thought hardly fits the context here, nor is it in agreement with the more frequent use of the word *inheritance* in the New Testament (see verse 14, v. 5 and Col. i. 12). The preposition (*en*) here has the force of

[1] W. M. F. Scott, *The Hidden Mystery* (1942), pp. 23f.

'among' as is clear from the two close parallels to the expression of this verse in Acts xx. 32 and xxvi. 18. The fellowship of Christians is the sphere in which the inheritance of God is found, just as it is true also that it is in and through His Church that the truth of God's purpose becomes known and declared (iii. 9–11 and 18). As men are enlightened by the Spirit of God, who is Himself the earnest of the inheritance (i. 14), so increasingly they realize *the riches* of that inheritance (see on verse 7), and its glory, that is, its essential quality as life in God for ever. It is to be noted also that just as it was *his calling* (not yours) of which the apostle spoke, so here it is *his inheritance*, the inheritance from God the Father which Christians share with His Son Jesus Christ (Rom. viii. 17).

19. Thirdly the apostle prays for enlightenment that, in addition to vision and aspiration, they may know *what is the exceeding greatness of his power*. Once again he expresses this in the strongest terms that language can find, both by speaking of its surpassing magnitude, and by using all the synonyms possible. The four words are distinguished more clearly as they are translated in RV as 'power', 'working', 'strength' and 'might'. The *power* (*dunamis*) of God he would stress in particular is not just an abstract quality, but it is known *according to* its *working* which can be seen and realized. The Greek word here is *energeia* from which our word 'energy' comes, and the phrase used here is found again in iii. 7, iv. 16, Philippians iii. 21 and Colossians i. 29. Moreover it is His great 'strength' (*kratos*), that distinctive attribute of the divine nature that is praised in the New Testament doxologies (1 Tim. vi. 16; 1 Pet. iv. 11, v. 11; Jude 25; Rev. i. 6, v. 13); and it is His 'might' (*ischus*) which He possesses and is also able to make available to us (cf. vi. 10; 1 Pet. iv. 11). The burden of the prayer in fact is that the mighty power of God may be known in experience by its operation *to us-ward who believe* (cf. iii. 20); and the apostle is confident that it belongs to men on this simple condition of their believing, that is, their laying hold of it, accepting it from Him, as a gift that He wants them to have.

20. The power which thus is made available to men is the power demonstrated, and known in its true measure, by God's own working, power *which he wrought in Christ*, and that in two decisive acts. First, He showed this power *when he raised him from the dead*. Most frequently the New Testament describes the resurrection as the work of God the Father (see Acts ii. 24, 32, etc.). His raising His Son from the dead is the mark of His approval, the acknowledgment of Him as His Son, and the declaration of Him as Lord of all (Acts iii. 15, iv. 10, x. 40, xvii. 31; Rom. i. 4). But it is also the manifestation of the Father's power. Secondly, that power is shown in that He *set him at his own right hand*. The ascension may not often be described in the New Testament (Mk. xvi. 19; Lk. xxiv. 51; Acts i. 9), but it is constantly assumed, and its significance stressed (e.g. Rom. viii. 34; Col. iii. 1; Heb. i. 3; 1 Pet. iii. 22). To Paul, and in the New Testament generally, the cross, the resurrection and the ascension are considered as three parts of one great act of God. The ascension, like the resurrection, is emphasized as being the Father's work. It is His honouring His Son with the highest possible honour (Phil. ii. 9–11), but, again, it is also the demonstration of His power.

In the words here we have an allusion to Psalm cx. 1, a verse often referred to in the New Testament. The exalting of the king of Israel as God's anointed lent itself to a supreme application to the Christ. It was so applied before His coming, but most especially after His death and resurrection and ascension (Acts ii. 34f.; Heb. i. 13; and see also Mt. xxvi. 64; Acts vii. 55; Rom. viii. 34; Col. iii. 1; Heb. i. 3, viii. 1, x. 12, xii. 2; 1 Pet. iii. 22). Inevitably as the ascension and exaltation of Christ are referred to we have spatial imagery, but as Calvin puts it, when it is said that He is lifted up to the Father's right hand, 'It does not mean any particular place, but the power which the Father hath bestowed on Christ, that he may administer in his name the government of heaven and earth.'

Thus the resurrection and ascension express the measure of the Father's power made available to men. The apostle prayed for himself 'that I may know him, and the power of his resurrection' (Phil. iii. 10). Often he thought of these mighty acts of God not only as the measure of the power that Christians can possess but as indicating the divine strength that can raise them to new life with Christ (1 Cor. vi. 14; 2 Cor. iv. 14; Col. ii. 12), and make them live *in the heavenly places* (see on verse 3) with Him. But this latter thought is developed more fully in the next section (ii. 6).

21. Now the thought of the resurrection and exaltation of Christ leads rather to the declaration of Him as Lord of all. His position is *far above all principality, and power, and might, and dominion.* Such was always His place in the universe, because He is eternally God the Son (Jn. iii. 31). To it He was exalted again after He had humbled Himself to assume our humanity (Eph. iv. 10). The titles in this verse may have been taken as those of the spiritual powers venerated by the Gnostic teachers who were opposed by the apostle in Colossians. Three of the four used here are found in the plural in Colossians i. 16, where it is being asserted that Christ is the Creator of every spiritual power there is. Here Paul is concerned to affirm that Christ is Lord over them all, over *every name that is named*, every dignity that is reverenced by man (cf. Phil. ii. 9). There are powers *not only in this world, but also in that which is to come*: the apostle would thus far agree with the Gnostics. But he would assert that none of these has any being apart from Christ; all of them that are evil have been vanquished by Him (Col. ii. 15), and all are subject to Him as Lord (cf. Rom. viii. 38; 1 Pet. iii. 22). Against the spiritual powers of evil the servant of Christ must do battle in his Master's strength (Eph. vi. 12), and also Paul will say that to 'the principalities and powers in heavenly places' the Church is uniquely to declare 'the manifold wisdom of God' (iii. 10).

This world is more strictly 'this age' (RV mg., NEB—the Greek is *aiōn*), but in the New Testament the two words are often interchangeable, and here certainly the word has no temporal force. The contrast between this age and the age to come was common in the Rabbis and often implied in the New Testament by the use of one term or the other (e.g. in Lk. xvi. 8, xx. 34; Rom. xii. 2; 1 Cor. ii. 6; Heb. vi. 5). Together they may, as here and in Matthew xii. 32, make an all-embracing whole.

22. What has gone before may be summed up by saying that the Father *hath put all things under his feet*, and so, doubtless intentionally, the words of Psalm viii. 6 are used. This verse is used again in 1 Corinthians xv. 27, and it is important to notice that the Psalm speaks of the place of man as God intended him to be, 'crowned . . . with glory and honour' and made 'to have dominion over the works' of God's hands. In a great measure man lost this position by the weakness and bondage into which he was brought by sin. Therefore we see One only, the true Man Christ Jesus, fulfilling this divine purpose; but through Him and in Him we are restored to our true dignity. Hebrews ii. 5–10 may be regarded as an inspired commentary on Psalm viii as fulfilled in Christ, and in those who through Him are brought as 'sons unto glory'.

Jesus Christ is Lord over all, but in particular this is His relationship to the Church, for the Father *gave him to be the head over all things to the church*. When He is spoken of as Head, sometimes the primary thought is of His Lordship, sometimes of His place with respect to the body, directing all the parts that are joined to Him as in an organic unity. In iv. 15 and in Colossians ii. 19 this latter is the primary thought. Here, the thought is first of His presiding over the Church (cf. v. 23 and Col. i. 18), and this then leads on to the Church being called the Body of Christ.

We should note, however, that the apostle does not simply speak of Him as given to be Head of the Church—Lord of all, and of the Church in particular—but that He is 'supreme head' (NEB) or more literally Head over all things 'to' or 'for' the Church. There is given to the Church, and for the Church's benefit, a Head who is also Head over all things. The Church has authority and power to overcome all opposition because her Leader and Head is Lord of all. Jesus Himself had authority because He was under the Father's authority; He was doing His will and therefore had all the authority of God (see Mt. viii. 9f., xi. 27; Jn. xvii. 2). Such authority He passes on to His disciples in as much as they go out in His name, in obedience to Him, and to do His work (Mt. xxviii. 18–20; Mk. iii. 14f.; Jn. xx. 21–23).

23. For the Church's benefit Christ is Head, and His great purpose for the Church and its relationship to Him is expressed by speaking of it as *his body*. This is a most revealing term for the Church, peculiarly Pauline (ii. 16, iv. 4, 12, 16, v. 30; Rom. xii. 5; 1 Cor. x. 17, xii. 27; Col. i. 24, ii. 19), though the essential truth behind its use is found in other New Testament writers. It means more than saying that the Church is the company of the disciples of Christ, the people of God; it expresses the essential union of His people with Him (as in the parable of the vine and the branches in John xv)—the same life of God flows through all; and it speaks of the whole as functioning in obedience to Him, carrying out His work in the world.

This designation of the function of the Church is amplified yet further; it is not only His body, it is intended to be *the fulness of him that filleth all in all*. We may paraphrase this by saying that it is God's purpose that the Church should be the full expression of Jesus Christ, who Himself fills everything there is. Colossians i. 19 and ii. 9 speak of all the divine fullness indwelling Christ Himself, that is to say He is filled by, and is the full expression of, the Godhead. Colossians ii. 10 continues 'in him ye are made full' (RV). In this sense Christians are intended to be 'filled unto all the fulness of God' (iii. 19, RV and compare Jn. i. 14, 16), that is, to receive the fullness of the attributes and gifts of God that it is possible for men to receive. In this same way iv. 13 describes the Christian's growth to spiritual maturity as development 'unto the measure of the stature of the fulness of Christ'.

Another interpretation of these words, understood by many ancient versions in their translation of the Greek, and followed by many commentators, is that in some sense the Church fills Christ, and He is made complete by the Church. Robinson paraphrases, 'so the Christ may have no part lacking, but may be wholly completed and fulfilled'. So Calvin says, 'Until he is united to us, the Son of God reckons himself in some sense imperfect.' There are several reasons for this being taken as the meaning. It is felt that it gives a truer meaning of the word *fulness (plērōma)*, that which fills, rather than that which is filled. Also the form of the participle translated *that filleth* by AV is the Greek middle or passive voice, and not active as is the verb in iv. 10. On the other hand the meaning of *plērōma* (by formation a *passive* noun) seems to be best taken from the passages quoted above, and in particular the phrase in iv. 13 strongly favours the sense in which we have taken it here. If the participle were passive we could not interpret as AV and RV do; but if middle, the meaning would be much the same as the active. As Moule puts it, the middle 'suggests intensity and richness of action; a power which is indeed living and life-giving' *(CB)*. Nowhere in the New Testament is it said that Christ finds His fullness and fulfilment in the Church. (The nearest that we come to such a concept is in Col. i. 24.[1]) The reverse is the more natural idea, Christ filling all things and bringing all things to completeness of being; this fits the context here better, and it is one of the great themes of this Epistle (i. 10, iv. 10, 13, 16). The sequence of thought here seems to be: by His resurrection and ascension Christ is exalted to be Lord of all, He is Head of all things for the Church; the Church is His Body intended to express Him in the world; more than that, the Church is intended to be a full expression of Him by being filled by Him whose purpose it is to fill everything[2] there is.[3]

[1] See Robinson, pp. 43f.

[2] There is also greater difficulty in the phrase *all in all* if the participle is taken as passive. In that case, it must be an adverbial accusative, but this is perhaps less likely when the phrase is so closely connected with the participle by being put between it and its article.

[3] Another alternative has been proposed that brings the expression here nearer to that of Colossians. It is to take the words *which is his body* as parenthetical. Then Christ Himself is being described as *the fulness of* God. NEB (in text) takes *plērōma* as passive, with reference to the Church, and the participle as also passive, but with reference to Christ: 'the church, which is his body and as such holds within it the fullness of him who himself receives the entire fullness of God'.

II. LIFE IN CHRIST (ii. 1–iii. 21)

a. New life from the dead (ii. 1–10)

1. The apostle's intercession has led him to speak of the power of God shown supremely in raising His Son Jesus Christ from the dead, and to pray that his readers may know spiritual power in their lives in such measure (i. 19f.). He has also spoken of their calling into His Body, the Church. He wants to demonstrate the great truth that Jew and Gentile are brought together into that Body. But before he does so he shows that both Jew and Gentile alike have now received new life in and with the risen Christ. This section is one long sentence and the AV, by printing the words *hath he quickened* in italics, indicates that the verb of the sentence does not belong to the text at this point. It comes only in verse 5, and is put here to make the sentence read more easily in English. In the original it begins with the object, *and you*, and as in the great exposition of salvation by Christ in Romans i–viii, the apostle does not show the grace of God until he has made inescapably clear the desperate need and universal sinfulness of man (cf. Col. i. 21, 22).

Man's trouble is not merely that he is out of harmony with his environment and with his fellows. He is 'alienated from the life of God' (iv. 18), that is, with respect to his true spiritual nature he is *dead in trespasses and sins*. There is probably no essential difference between the two nouns; the root meaning of the first is 'missing the mark' and of the second 'slipping' or 'falling from the way', and thus both express man's failure to live as he could and ought. Men were made in God's image to live as children in His family, aware of His presence, rejoicing in His direction. Freedom was given, but with it a warning that it involved the possibility of disobedience, and that disobedience would lead to death (Gn. ii. 17). This death is not primarily physical death, but the loss of the spiritual life given, life in fellowship with God and the consequent capacity for spiritual activity and development. Thus the description here is not merely metaphorical, nor does it refer only to the future state of the sinner. It describes his present condition, and the Bible indeed often thus speaks of man in a state of spiritual death because of sin (e.g. Ezk. xxxvii. 1–14; Rom. vi. 23, vii. 10, 24; Col. ii. 13), and needing nothing less than new life from God (cf. Eph. v. 14; Jn. iii. 3, v. 24).

2. Man's sinful condition is lifeless and motionless as far as any Godward activity is concerned. Viewed from another standpoint it is a *walk*, a taking of step after step, in evil (cf. iv. 17). The Jews called their laws of conduct *Halachah*, which means 'Walking' (cf. Mk. vii. 5; Acts xxi. 21; Heb. xiii. 9, RV mg.). The figure is used later in this letter (ii. 10, iv. 1, v. 2, 8, 15), as elsewhere in the New Testament (e.g. 2 Cor. v. 7; Col. iv. 5; 1 Jn. i. 6; 2 Jn. 4) for the progress of the Christian life; but here it describes a life lived according to an authority contrary to God.

This authority is expressed in three ways, in terms of its power in the world, its spiritual nature, and its activity in men's lives. First, it is that which is in accordance with *the course of this world*. One or other of these two words, *aiōn* translated *course* or more often 'age', and *kosmos* translated *world*, is often used in the New Testament to contrast the life of men apart from God, limited by earthbound motives, with that life which is lived in acknowledgment of the kingship of God and with the realization of His presence (see on i. 21). Doubtless the two words are used together for emphasis here. We might render the phrase as 'the spirit of this age'.

Then secondly, it is *according to the prince of the power of the air*. By this phrase, grammatically difficult in the original, but essentially clear in meaning, the devil is described; and by speaking of the devil's authority as 'in the air', Paul was not necessarily accepting the current notion of the air being the abode and realm of evil spirits. Basically his thought was of an evil power with control in the world (see on vi. 12), but whose existence was not material but spiritual.

In the third place, Paul speaks of the authority of *the spirit that now worketh in the children of disobedience*. In this phrase there is another grammatical difficulty, but whether *spirit* depends as a genitive on *prince* or *power*, the essential meaning is clear. The old life, without the energizing of God (see i. 11 and 20) is subject to the energizing (Gk. *energountos*) of the powers of evil, controlled by the spirit which has the evil one as its source. For man's inner life must be surrendered to the working of God or to that of the powers of evil (cf. Lk. xxii. 3; Jn. xiii. 2, 27; Acts v. 4; and especially see Lk. xi. 24–26). And if men are surrendered to the power of evil, they become those whose habit of life is contrary to the living God, and so they are rightly called *the children of disobedience* (cf. v. 8).

3. The apostle has begun to speak of Gentiles, but now he changes to the first person (see on i. 11) and so includes himself and *all* his people as *among* the children of disobedience (cf. Rom. ii. 1–9, iii. 9, 23). An alternative way of taking the relative here is with reference to trespasses and sins 'in which', he may have intended to say, *we all had our conversation in times past*. Essentially it makes little difference to the meaning. The old way of life was a life in sin and disobedience following *the lusts of the flesh*. The word 'flesh', as used in the New Testament, signifies in the first place simply the matter of the body, not inherently evil—the Word of God could become flesh (Jn. i. 14). Then it could be used to speak of the whole lower nature of man, apart from the regenerating and sanctifying Spirit of God. The biblical phrase 'the lusts of the flesh' is not to be taken in too narrow a sense, but as the longings and impulses of the self-centred life (cf. Rom. viii. 4–9; Gal. v. 16–21). Apart from his restoration to God and the indwelling of God's Spirit, man is not only dominated by self-centred passions, but he is found actually *fulfilling the desires of the flesh and of the mind*. This last word, a plural of a word more commonly used in the singular (*dianoia*) meaning a 'thought' or 'purpose', or 'intelligence', signifies clearly that the effects of man's evil and selfishness are not limited to the emotions but embrace his intellect and reasoning processes as well (cf. Col. i. 21). RSV translates the whole phrase 'following the desires of body and mind'.

Paul says finally that Jews, *even as others* (literally 'the rest', *hoi loipoi*, as many of his own people disparagingly called the Gentiles), *were by nature the children of wrath*. Many have taken this to mean that we were born with a nature that made us, even before we actually sinned, subject to the wrath of God. We would have therefore in the verse not only a doctrine of 'original sin' but of 'original guilt' or 'transmitted guilt'. It is argued on the other hand that neither of the phrases *children of wrath* and *by nature* refers necessarily to the condition of men dating back to birth. *Children* here characterizes people of a certain type without special reference of necessity to their parentage or to what they have inherited from their parents; in this Epistle alone we have 'children of disobedience' (ii. 2) and 'children of light' (v. 8), and the New Testament provides other similar examples. *By nature* often refers to what is innate, to what a person is by virtue of his birth (Rom. ii. 27, xi. 24; Gal. ii. 15), but this is not always the case. Romans ii. 14, for example, shows that it can mean what people are by the habitual practices of their lives, what they are if left to themselves, not necessarily because of the inborn nature. So NEB takes it here, 'In our natural condition we, like the rest, lay under the dreadful judgment of God.' Furthermore, it is asked whether what is logically prior—if 'transmitted guilt' was intended—would be set thus at the end. Instead the regular biblical order is seen—the sin of man, in thought and in action, and in consequence the wrath of God. In fact we have here in just a few clauses a summing up of Paul's great treatment of sin and its consequences in Romans i–iii. Jew and Gentile alike have sinned against the light and the law that they have possessed and known, and so 'all the world' are 'brought under the judgement of God' (Rom. iii. 19, RV).

4. Such was the plight of all mankind. *But God* broke in. In strong contrast to the need and sinfulness of man, and meeting that need and sinfulness, there comes the fact of God's love, and the action that springs from His pity. The subject of the verb has waited from the beginning of the chapter to this point. The verb waits till the next verse, till Paul in his usual manner (cf. i. 17, iii. 9, 15f.), having mentioned the name of God, speaks in glowing terms of His goodness and grace. He is not only merciful, showing His pity to those who are totally unworthy and undeserving; He is *rich in mercy* (see on i. 7). That mercy proceeds from love, *his great love wherewith he loved us*. There is longing in the heart of God for men—the *us* now means Jews and Gentiles alike—to be restored to the highest and best that He had planned for them (cf. Jn. iii. 16; 1 Jn. iv. 9f.); and so He has shown Himself full of mercy, and has acted in grace towards them.

5. But before the apostle describes the action of the love of God, he resumes the object and emphasizes once again man's condition and desperate need. His love reached down to us *even when we were dead in sins* (cf. Rom. v. 6, 8), and He *quickened us together with Christ*. We have seen that new life, and nothing less, was man's need. By His death and resurrection He did no less than bring 'life and immortality to light' (2 Tim. i. 10). For in His death He suffered for sin, and removed the barrier to fellowship with God that sin caused, and by His resurrection He showed His triumph over death, physical and spiritual. Thus the forgiveness of sins, as Colossians ii. 13 indicates, means that new life can be received. Because Christ was raised from the dead, men are raised from being dead in sins, and have new life with Christ and in Christ (cf. Rom. vi. 4–8, viii. 11; 2 Cor. iv. 14). The word *together*, here and twice in the next verse, is given in the Greek by adding the prepositional prefix *sun-* to the verb. Often Paul used it thus to express a union with Christ (cf. Rom. vi. 6, 8; Col. ii. 12; 2 Tim. ii. 11f.), and in this case it led him apparently to coin a new word to express the new revelation. The preposition here may also carry the hint of the fact that from whatever racial or national background men have come, they are brought into this new life in Christ in fellowship together, a theme that is developed fully in the next section.[1]

This new life, as the exposition of it has shown, can also be described as salvation from sin, and Paul cannot help but add

---

[1] It would be necessary to take this as the force of the compound verb if the variant reading with 'in' before 'Christ' were accepted. In the next verse the phrase 'in Christ Jesus' certainly follows verbs compounded with *sun-*, but probably the true reading in this verse omits 'in'.

here (though he waits till later to develop it) his favourite summing up of the gospel, *by grace ye are saved*. For man's position could be described not only in terms of spiritual death, but also as enslavement and inescapable entanglement in the coils of sin. From that bondage Christ set men free (cf. Rom. vi. 12–23). The precise form of words here stresses two things. As consistently emphasized by Paul, it is entirely of His *grace*, His free, undeserved favour to mankind. Then also this salvation is presented as an accomplished fact. There are ways in which the New Testament can speak of salvation as a present (1 Cor. i. 18, xv. 2; 2 Cor. ii. 15) or a future experience (Rom. v. 9f.), since it means deliverance from the power of sin now, and in the end it will mean deliverance from the very presence of sin. But as deliverance from the penalty of sin, as free forgiveness, salvation is described by the use of the perfect tense, expressing as it does a completed action, 'continuous and permanent' in its results (Robinson). 'By grace have ye been saved' RV more accurately translates.

6. In i. 20 we read of the declaration of the Father's power, not only in raising Christ from the dead, but also in the fact that He 'set him at his own right hand in the heavenly places'. So, as this chapter speaks of His quickening us together with Christ, it goes on to say that He *hath raised us up together, and made us sit together in heavenly places in Christ Jesus*. In i. 3 the apostle has said that God has 'blessed us with all spiritual blessings in heavenly places in Christ'. Now he says more specifically that our life has come to be there, enthroned with Christ. If this is not explicitly stated elsewhere in the Pauline Epistles, the meaning is implicit in such a passage as Colossians iii. 1–3. Man, by virtue of Christ's conquest of sin and death and by His exaltation, is lifted 'from the deepest hell to heaven itself' (Calvin). His citizenship is now in heaven (Phil. iii. 20); and there, and not under the limits imposed by the world, nor in conformity to its standards (Rom. xii. 2), he is to find his true life.

7. The purpose of God for His Church, as Paul came to

understand it, reaches beyond itself, beyond the salvation, the enlightenment and the re-creation of individuals, beyond its unity and fellowship, beyond even its witness to the world. The Church is to be the exhibition to the whole creation of the wisdom and love and grace of God in Christ. (The verb used, *endeiknumi*, means 'display' (NEB) or *shew* rather than simply 'make known', as its use in such passages as Rom. ii. 15 and Tit. iii. 2 indicates.) This has been expressed in part in i. 6, 12 and 14 where the spiritual blessings that come to men in Christ were spoken of as given and received 'to the praise of the glory of his grace'. It will be expressed more specifically in iii. 9, 10. Here the purpose of our being raised to new life in Christ, and lifted with Him to a heavenly citizenship, is said to be *that in the ages to come he might shew the exceeding riches of his grace in his kindness toward us through Christ Jesus.*

Sometimes *the ages to come* have been understood to refer to successive stages or periods of this present world order. The language, though this phrase is not paralleled precisely in the New Testament, is against this. (See on i. 21 and cf. Mt. xii. 32; Mk. x. 30.) Paul never saw this world order as such an extending vista with successive ages. It is true that in his later Epistles he placed less stress on the immediacy of Christ's coming again, perhaps as he saw the vastness of the unfinished task, but he never exchanged the sense of urgency for a concept of unrolling ages between himself and the Lord's coming, nor did he vary his emphasis on the need for preparedness to meet the Lord at any time (see Phil. i. 10, ii. 16, iii. 20, iv. 5 and Col. iii. 4). We must allow iii. 10 to help interpret this verse. The apostle's vision of the function of the Church in the purpose of God has been lifted beyond this present order; it is the life to come, and not this life, which he thought of in terms of unfolding ages.

We should notice further that here again the word *grace* demanded qualification in terms that could show the wonder of the God who is its author (cf. i. 7f. and ii. 4). Once more there are shown to be riches of grace, the true eternal wealth (see on i. 7), exceeding, abounding, overflowing riches (the participle has been used of the power of God in i. 19) displayed towards mankind in Christ.[1] That grace, moreover, is expressed in *kindness (chrēstotēs)*, a word that denotes love in action (cf. Rom. ii. 4, xi. 22; Tit. iii. 4), personal pity and help rendered as man needed it most.

8. Now the statement made parenthetically in verse 5 is repeated, expanded and expounded. Why can man possess the life of heaven here and now? How is there such an exhibition of the love of God from which the whole creation of God can learn and wonder? Because 'by grace have ye been saved' (RV). This salvation is God's work entirely, the bestowal of His infinite love. The part of men in receiving it can be described simply by the words *through faith* (cf. Rom. iii. 22, 25; Gal. ii. 16; 1 Pet. i. 5). And this faith is defined best as a turning to God with a sense of need and weakness and emptiness and a willingness to receive what He offers, to receive the Lord Himself (Jn. i. 12).

Anxious to emphasize with crystal clarity the nature of this faith and the nature of grace, Paul, by his qualifying phrases in this verse and the next, excludes the possibility of man's obtaining this salvation by any merit or effort of his own. First he adds to his statement of salvation by grace through faith the words *and that not of yourselves: it is the gift of God.* Sometimes this has been taken to mean that the faith is not of man, but God's gift. If we take it in this way, we would need to regard the second part of verse 8 as a parenthesis—verse 9 must refer to the salvation and not to faith. It seems better, however, especially in the light of the parallelism between verse 8 and verse 9 (*not of yourselves* . . . 'not of works') to take all the qualifying clauses as in contrast to salvation by grace. What the apostle wants to say is that the whole initiative and every aspect of the making available of this salvation is God's. 'God's is the gift' is the rendering that shows best the emphasis of the word order in the Greek. 'Let a man be abandoned by God, and he is absolutely hopeless. It is the voice of God that arouses, that awakens, that causes a man to think and enquire; it is the power of God that gives strength to act; it is

[1] The RV 'in' rather than AV *through Christ* is right.

the same power which makes provision for the need of the new life.'[1]

9. Then, secondly, we are taken back to the terminology of Romans and Galatians, and to what was a vital question for the Jews of Paul's day because of their exaltation of the law. But such is the heart of man, and so great is man's temptation in every age and race to deceive himself into thinking that his life is good enough for God, that the reminder of this verse is needed still. If this salvation is of God's grace and received by men simply through faith, it is *not of works* (Rom. iii. 20, 28, iv. 1–5; Gal. ii. 16; 2 Tim. i. 9; Tit. iii. 5). For 'all have sinned', and suffer sin's consequences, the exclusion from life in fellowship with God. From man's side no-one, except one without sin, could restore himself or any other into a position of acceptance with God. This means furthermore that no-one can *boast* before God, since all are admitted on the grounds of grace. 'Some room', says Calvin, 'must always remain for man's boasting, so long as, independently of grace, merits are of any avail.' But merits have no place. God will allow no-one to boast (cf. Rom. iii. 27). The words here may in fact imply that this was a part of God's purpose and the reason for His bringing salvation as He did, to exclude man's pride (cf. Jdg. vii. 2). Or perhaps we should take it simply as a result, 'There is nothing for anyone to boast of' (NEB). In either case it is made clear that the only right attitude, the only possible attitude for sinful men before their Maker and their Judge is penitence and humble dependence. Their only pride can be in the cross by which they find salvation (Gal. vi. 14) and in the Saviour who suffered there (1 Cor. i. 29–31; Phil. iii. 3ff.).

10. The work of God for mankind in Christ has been described as the gift of new life, and as the gift of salvation. Now it is shown further that man of himself could have no part in it by its being described as a new creation. *We*, in this new life, this

[1] C. Brown, *St. Paul's Epistle to the Ephesians. A Devotional Commentary* (1911), p. 48.

new nature that we have received, are *his workmanship*. The Greek again gains emphasis by the order of words, as it makes the *his* stand first in the sentence. The noun used (*poiēma*) is of a different root from the *works* (*ergōn*) of the previous verse, and is found elsewhere in the New Testament only in Romans i. 20, where it is used of the works of God's first creation. Man was His making at the first, and now, because that work of His was spoilt by sin, there is a new divine act of creation. For 'if any man is in Christ, he is a new creature' (2 Cor. v. 17, RV —see also Eph. iv. 24; Gal. vi. 15; Col. iii. 10). *In Christ Jesus*— the phrase comes for the third time in five verses—in faith-union with Him, men whose lives were marred and ruined by failure and sin are made new.

'Works' have been excluded as a means of amassing merit and gaining favour with God. The gulf between God and man must be bridged by God's action. The new life in fellowship with God must be God's creation and cannot be man's work. But nevertheless the essential quality of the new life is *good works*. The preposition here (Gk. *epi*, AV *unto*, RV and RSV 'for') shows that more is involved than saying that good works were the purpose of the new life, or that men were redeemed in order to be a people 'zealous of good works' (Tit. ii. 14; cf. Col. i. 10); rather it is that good works are 'involved' in the new life 'as an inseparable condition' (Abbott). His new creation must be spoken of as being 'in righteousness and true holiness' (Eph. iv. 24). It is of such a kind that it must and will express itself in this way.

To demonstrate this still further as being the divine purpose Paul adds concerning such good works that God has *before ordained* (RV 'afore prepared') *that we should walk in them*. This does not of necessity mean that there are particular good works that are God's purpose for us. There can be no objection to such a concept, if it is reckoned that the foreknowledge of an almighty and omniscient God is not opposed to His gift of free will to men. But probably it is rather the whole course of life that is in view here. The nature and character of the works and the direction of the Christian's daily *walk* (see on ii. 2) are predetermined. This then corresponds closely with i. 4

which describes the end and goal of election as 'that we should be holy and without blame before him'.

b. The reconciliation of Jews and Gentiles (ii. 11–22)

11. The purpose of Christ's work for man's salvation is not limited to the giving of new life to individual men and women, previously dead in sin, as the last section has described. Chapter i has given hints that it goes beyond this, and the present section now shows that it involves the bringing of those individuals, whatever their race or background, into unity in the people of God. In this respect it involves the greatest transformation of situation for the Gentiles, and this section, like verses 1–10, begins by showing what was the condition of Gentiles in the past, calling them to *remember*, and thus be stirred to love and gratitude. First they should think of the great change that has come in their relationship with the Jews, their connection with those who were named the people of God. Just as the Greeks despised those who lived outside of their cities, calling them *ethnē* (pagans), so the Jews in their superficial and unspiritual way of thinking (*in the flesh*), instead of regarding the other nations as those with whom they should have shared their knowledge of God (cf. Gn. xii. 3; Is. xlii. 1, 6, xlix. 6), simply spoke disparagingly of them as *Gentiles (ethnē)*.[1] They called them the *Uncircumcision*, the men who did not have on them the mark of the covenant of God with His people. This was the proud judgment of those who called themselves the *Circumcision*, though from the standpoint of the man in Christ this mark might be only *in the flesh made by hands*.

Elsewhere in the Pauline Epistles we find this contrast between the circumcision which is of the Spirit and that which is merely of the flesh, a work of men's hands; and we may compare the way in which the tabernacle and temple are so described in the New Testament (Mk. xiv. 58; Acts vii. 48; Heb. ix. 11, 24) when contrasted with the spiritual temple as Paul speaks of it here in verse 21. Paul did not disparage

[1] Barclay (p. 125) well illustrates the extreme forms that the Jewish contempt for the Gentiles could take.

circumcision as an institution. It was to him the God-given
sign of the covenant; but if the outward sign was not matched
by an inward faith and an obedience of life to the covenant,
it became worthless and just a work of the flesh (1 Cor. vii. 19;
Gal. v. 6, vi. 15). The circumcision that mattered, whether or
not there was any outward sign, was the spiritual circumcision,
a putting off of sin and an obedience to Christ (Rom. ii.
25–29; Phil. iii. 2f.; Col. ii. 11).

12. The fundamental change for the Gentiles, however,
was not simply in the way that the Jews regarded them, but in
their actual condition. Their lack of privilege and opportunity
may be described in the far-reaching terms of this verse. *At
that time*, before they came to know and experience the grace
of God, they *were without Christ*. These words may stand as the
first description of the position of the Gentiles (RV), or, more
likely, as the basic one on which the others depend (AV). In
the latter case we may see this whole section as drawing out
the contrast between what the Gentiles were without the hope
of the Messiah, and all that went with that, and what they
came to be 'in Christ Jesus' (verse 13).

They were *aliens from the commonwealth of Israel*. They did not
belong to, and found themselves cut off from, the fellowship
and the privileges (such as Rom. iii. 1f. and ix. 4f. describe)
of those who truly called themselves the people of God. The
word used for *aliens* is that used in iv. 18 and Colossians i. 21
for man's separation from God by sin. The only other New
Testament use of the word translated *commonwealth* is in Acts
xxii. 28 where it refers to the much-coveted Roman citizenship. Whatever purpose of God for the Gentiles may have been
expressed in the Old Testament, in actual fact they stood
almost entirely outside the spiritual privileges of Israel. The
Jews did admit Gentiles as proselytes, it is true, but the way of
entry was difficult, and even then the sense of alienation was
not fully removed. In particular they were *strangers from the
covenants of promise*. The promise to the Jews, *the* promise of the
Messiah (Greek has the article), was involved in the covenants
with Abraham and the patriarchs (Gn. xvii. 1–14, xxvi. 24,

xxviii. 13–15), and with the nation under Moses (Ex. xxiv. 1–11). The covenants brought Israel into a special relationship of grace with God, and so to the hope of a deliverance and future glory that would be theirs. But up till this time the Gentiles had not been included within these covenants. So they stood as a people with *no hope*.

In fact they were not only without the hope that Israel had, but they were without any real hope at all. This was a very evident characteristic of the Gentile world of the time when Jesus came. They had no prospect for the future, no assurance of life beyond this. The Greeks, for example, looked back on a golden age in the past rather than to a future glory; or more philosophically they took a cyclic view of history. There was in consequence no concept of a goal to which all things were moving, and this lack of hope was seen most notably in their view of death.

Finally, Paul says that they were *without God*. The Greek word here (*atheoi*) does not mean that they refused to believe in God, or that they were forsaken by God, or godless in their conduct, but that they had no real knowledge of God. In most cases they had many objects of worship—'gods many, and lords many'—but they were gods in name only (1 Cor. viii. 4f.; Gal. iv. 8). Some sought for the One in philosophy; some tried to come within the fold of Judaism. But by and large the Gentiles had to live *in the world* lives limited by the things of the world, and had to face the trials and sorrows and perplexities of the world without the knowledge of God to interpret the whole.

13. Now, however, for these Gentiles, everything had become different, because from being 'without Christ' (verse 12), they had come to be *in Christ Jesus*—they had come to find their life in Him. They who had been *far off*—far from God, and with a great gulf dividing them from His covenant people—were *made nigh*. The Rabbis had a way of speaking of Gentiles who were far from the privileges of the covenant being 'made nigh' as proselytes.[1] But Paul is speaking of a far

[1] See quotations from the rabbinical writings in Abbott, p. 60.

more fundamental and wonderful way of approach *by the blood of Christ* (see on i. 7). For the basic cause of man's estrangement is his sin, and Christ gave Himself as a sacrifice for the sins of the whole world (Jn. iii. 16, xii. 32; 2 Cor. v. 19; 1 Jn. ii. 2). The sins of both Jews and Gentiles can be forgiven because of His death, and both can be brought near to God as never before, and so brought near to each other. Divisions are overcome, not by an approaching or a receiving on either side, but by Christ coming and making peace for both.

14. Not only can it be said that Christ brings peace. *He is our peace.* As men are brought to be in Him, and continue to live in Him, they find peace with God, and so also a meeting-place and concord with one another, whatever may have been their divisions of race, colour, class or creed before. He came for this purpose (Lk. ii. 14), to be the Prince of peace, and indeed in such terms the prophets had foretold His coming (Is. ix. 6f., liii. 5; Mi. v. 5; Hg. ii. 9; Zc. ix. 10). By His coming, and supremely by His cross, He has *made both one.* The Greek says literally that He has made both things into one thing (later, in verse 15, the personal is used). The organization of Judaism and that of the Gentile world no longer stand apart as before. Divisions and distinctions no longer exist as far as the standing of any before God is concerned. God has made a way for the divided to become one (cf. Jn. x. 16, xvii. 11; 1 Cor. x. 17, xii. 13).

Paul is pre-occupied, however, with what to him was the greatest division of all, that which separated Jews and Gentiles. There had always been a *middle wall of partition*, a dividing wall, between the two. There was a barrier both literally and spiritually. In Jerusalem, between the temple proper and the Court of the Gentiles, there was a stone wall on which there was an inscription in Greek and Latin 'which forbade any foreigner to go in, under pain of death'.[1] It is strangely significant that Paul was finally arrested and condemned by

---

[1] Josephus in his *Antiquities* xv. 11. 5 and *The Wars of the Jews* v. 5. 2, vi. 2. 4 tells of this, and such an inscription was discovered by the French archaeologist M. Clermont Ganneau in 1871.

the Jews in Jerusalem on the basis of a false accusation that he took an Ephesian, Trophimus, beyond this barrier (Acts xxi. 29f.). But Christ had now *broken down* the barrier between Jews and Gentiles, of which that dividing wall in the temple was a symbol.

15. In order, however, that that particular dividing wall between Jews and Gentiles might be broken down, two things closely connected in the minds of strict Jews had to be dealt with. The old *enmity* had to go. The feeling of animosity and hostility had to be replaced by a sense of fellowship. Secondly, *the law of commandments contained in ordinances* had to be *abolished* (cf. Col. ii. 14, 20). This phrase should perhaps be taken as qualifying *the enmity*, or it may be that *the enmity* should be taken with the earlier participle, as describing the middle wall of partition. In fact the law with its detailed ordinances of ceremonies and regulations about the clean and the unclean had the effect of imposing a barrier and of causing enmity between Jews and Gentiles.

Because Christ has come, and by what He has done *in his flesh*, especially by His death (see Col. i. 22), salvation and acceptance with God in His people is offered to all men on condition of repentance and faith. Peter was sent to Cornelius and bidden to regard no longer the distinction between ceremonial cleanness and uncleanness (Acts x). The Church in its council at Jerusalem had agreed that there was no longer to be a barrier because the Jews had circumcision and all the other ordinances of the law, and the Gentiles did not (Acts xv). The Lord came not to destroy the law, but to fulfil (Mt. v. 17). Much of it (e.g. the sacrificial ritual) was preparation for, and foreshadowing of, the Christ, and so was fulfilled by what He did when He came. The moral demands and principles of the law were not lightened by Jesus, but made fuller and more far-reaching (Mt. v. 21–48). In the discipline of obedience that its detailed regulations demanded, and as the revealer of right and wrong, it was intended to lead to Christ (Gal. iii. 24). In an absolute sense it cannot be said to be made of no effect in Christ (Rom. iii. 31). But as a code 'specific, rigid, and outward, fulfilled in external ordinances' (Westcott), and so serving to separate Jews and Gentiles, it was abolished (cf. Col. ii. 20–22).

The Lord's coming meant *making peace* between Jew and Gentile, by taking away the cause of division. The law could no longer be the way by which Jews, and Jews alone, could try to come to God. The way of approach is now by grace, by a new creative work of God, the same for both Jews and Gentiles. The purpose of Christ is 'to create out of the two a single new humanity in himself' (NEB). *In* Christ—the phrase comes again—there is a new humanity; and it is a single entity. God now deals with Jews and Gentiles as a single individual. Furthermore, Gentiles do not simply rise to the status of Jews, but both become something *new* and greater; and it is significant that the word for *new* here (*kainos*) means not simply new in point of time, but as Barclay puts it 'new in the sense that it brings into the world a new kind of thing, a new quality of thing, which did not exist before' (see also on iv. 23f.).

16. Right through this passage the twin themes of the reconciliation of men to God, and of men to one another, are inextricably intertwined. *By the cross* the purpose of Christ was to *reconcile* men *unto God* (cf. Rom. v. 10; 2 Cor. v. 18–20; Col. i. 20). When He was slain there *the enmity* between man and God through sin was *slain*, because He bore man's sins and made possible his forgiveness. He thus reconciled *both* Jew and Gentile to God, but also He reconciled them (and people of all the different divisions of mankind) to one another and brought them to be *in one body*, thus putting to death *the enmity* between them. What He has done once and for all 'in the body of his flesh through death' (Col. i. 22), He now effects in the *one body* which is His Church. But here we should note that the emphasis is not quite that of i. 23 on the Church as *Christ's* Body, but rather on the fact that there is one living organism in which members so diverse belong together (cf. iv. 4; 1 Cor. x. 17, xii. 13; Col. iii. 15).

17, 18. The same linking of the thought of man's new relationship to God and to his fellows continues in these next two verses. The coming of Christ meant that *peace* could be *preached* to them *which were afar off*, the Gentiles, who previously had 'no hope' and were 'without God in the world', and *to them that were nigh*, the Jews who had 'the covenants of promise' and belonged to the people of God (cf. Dt. iv. 7; Ps. cxlviii. 14). For both this was peace with God, which both equally needed; and its consequence was peace and concord one with the other as well. In the words of this verse there is an allusion (as perhaps also in verse 13) to Isaiah lvii. 19, and probably also to Isaiah lii. 7 which speaks of the preaching of peace. These Old Testament passages (referred to also in Acts ii. 39 and Rom. x. 15) did not originally speak of the way of peace for the Gentiles, but such words of Scripture, deeply imprinted on the apostle's mind, found an apt application to this wonderful new situation. The form of expression, thus dependent on the Old Testament words, is not to be pressed too far. We are not to ask what preaching of the gospel of peace this refers to—before or after the resurrection, before or after Pentecost. The point is that Christ came 'with a gospel of peace' (Moffatt). Through His cross peace was made, and He through His Church takes out the message of reconciliation and peace to the world (cf. Acts x. 36; 2 Cor. v. 18–20).

Then further, the apostle says, *through him*, Christ Jesus, we have *access . . . unto the Father*. Access is probably the best translation of *prosagōgē*, though it could be 'introduction'. In oriental courts there was a *prosagōgēs* who brought a person into the presence of the king. The thought could be of Christ as the *prosagōgēs*, but the form of expression in the whole clause suggests rather that by Him there is a way of approach (cf. iii. 12). He is the Door, the Way to the Father (Jn. x. 7, 9, xiv. 6); by Him men, though sinners, because they are reconciled can 'come boldly unto the throne of grace' (Heb. iv. 16). But it is added that the *access* is for *both* Jew and Gentile in *one Spirit* (cf. 1 Cor. xii. 13). There is one way for all, one Spirit by whose work in their hearts they have assurance that they can come to God as children to a Father (Rom. viii. 15f.;

Gal. iv. 6). The personal Spirit of God is obviously intended here, and the form of the phrase should be noted. As Paul repeatedly uses the words 'in Christ' in this Epistle, so a number of times he says 'in the Spirit', to emphasize that for the new life of the Christian 'the Spirit is, as it were, the surrounding, sustaining power' (Westcott).

19. The unity of all Christians 'in one Spirit' will find emphasis and development in chapter iv, but now the apostle turns back specifically to the Gentiles to speak further of the change in their status and position. Before they were 'aliens from the commonwealth of Israel' (verse 12). In relation to the covenant people of God, they were *strangers* and pilgrims (*xenoi* and *paroikoi*), that is, people who might live alongside them in the same country, but without more than the most superficial rights of citizenship. Such was their old position, but it is so *no more*. Now, the apostle says, *ye are fellow-citizens with the saints*. His mind might have gone to the *saints* of Old Testament times, or to members of the Christian Church to all of whom the word applied (see on i. 1); probably he thought of all who in any sense could be called the people of God, and so he said to the Gentiles that they were now included among them, and on equal terms.

Citizenship of the people of God was one expressive way of telling the truth concerning the position in God's kingdom that Jews and Gentiles now equally share. But this figure had to give way to one that connoted a further truth, and could speak of the greater intimacy that Christians have with God, and indeed one with another. Jews and Gentiles, men of whatever race or colour or class, are together *of the household of God*, of the same family. Galatians vi. 10 uses the same word *oikeioi*, speaking of 'the household of faith'. Although the word does not fully express the truth that all are 'children of God by faith in Christ Jesus' (Gal. iii. 26; and see on i. 5), yet the thought is of the people of the household rather than the building (cf. Heb. iii. 2, 5f.; 1 Pet. iv. 17).

20. In what follows now, however, there are truths that can be conveyed best by the figure of the house (*oikos*) as a building. They whose faith is in Christ Jesus are like an edifice *built* (*epoikodomēthentes*) *upon the foundation of the apostles and prophets*. The question is asked whether this does not go against the Pauline figure of the house in 1 Corinthians iii. 11, where it is said that 'there can be no other foundation beyond that which is already laid . . . Jesus Christ himself' (NEB). To overcome the assumed difficulty some have suggested that we should take the words here to mean the foundation on which apostles and prophets were built, the foundation that they laid in the lives of others, or that they had built on in their work. We need not feel that this is necessary. What we have here we may regard simply as a slightly different handling of the same metaphor as that in 1 Corinthians iii. (Compare Rev. xxi. 14 for a use that is different again but not contradictory.) There the apostle thought of himself and others as builders, here as stones in the building. As Allan puts it, 'The Church rests on the total unique Event of which Christ is the centre, but in which the apostles and prophets, filled and guided by the Spirit and doing their work in unique closeness to Christ, had an indispensable and untransmissible part.' To apostles and prophets the word of God in Christ was revealed in a unique way (cf. iii. 5). Because they received, believed and witnessed to that word, they were the beginning of the building on which others were to be built (cf. Mt. xvi. 16–18). That the prophets of the Christian Church and not of the Old Testament are intended here is clear from the order of the phrase *apostles and prophets*, and by comparison with the use of the same phrase in iii. 5. (For the work of these Christian prophets see on iv. 11.)

As the building metaphor is applied here *Jesus Christ himself* is described as *the chief corner stone*, or, more exactly, simply 'the corner stone' (see Robinson). This thought comes from Psalm cxviii. 22, a passage which was used by our Lord Himself (Mk. xii. 10), and then in the early Church (Acts iv. 11; 1 Pet. ii. 7), 'The very stone which the builders rejected has become the head of the corner' (RSV). It denotes primarily the honour of His position in the building, but then also the way in which each stone is fitted into Him, and finds its true place and usefulness only in relation to Him (cf. Col. ii. 7; 1 Pet. ii. 4f.). There is some difference of opinion as to the precise place of the corner stone in the building, but it seems most likely that it was the stone set in the foundations at the corner to bind all together and to give the walls their line. Isaiah xxviii. 16, which is quoted together with Psalm cxviii. 22 in 1 Peter ii, speaks of the stone laid in Zion as 'a precious corner stone of sure foundation' (RV). Thus also Paul removes from this description any possible thought of the Lord Himself as Foundation being replaced by the apostles.

21, 22. Whatever the precise position of the corner stone, the main point of the metaphor is made explicit when it is said now that in Christ all that is built into the edifice is *fitly framed together*. Each finds his true place and function in relation to Christ and as he is built into Him. *All the building* is not strictly correct as a translation, since there is no article in the original. A more accurate translation would be 'every building' or 'each several building' (RV); but while this is a more exact rendering it is hardly true to the apostle's thought to suggest that the Church is as a number of different buildings. The word used (*oikodomē*) has a wide range of meaning. It is used sometimes for individual buildings (e.g. in Mk. xiii. 1f.), but very often in the New Testament for the whole work of building, and hence in the spiritual sense of 'edification' (as in iv. 12, 16, 29). It is the whole operation of building that is in view here (and probably similarly in 1 Cor. iii. 9), as the present participle 'being fitly framed together', and then the verb that follows, indicate. So we may say 'everything that is being built', or as Phillips puts it 'each separate piece of building'.

The work is developing; the Church cannot be described as a complete edifice until the final day of the Lord comes (cf. Rev. xxi). It is growing towards what it is intended to be in the purpose of God. The metaphor really breaks down at this point. There must be the thought of organic growth; the stones are 'living stones' (1 Pet. ii. 5, RV). To express this the description of the Church as a living body is preferable (as in iv. 15f.).

But the metaphor of the building has not been exhausted, and what is probably the chief reason for its use is not yet expressed. There is an analogy that can be drawn from the Old Testament that conveys a deep truth; this building *groweth unto an holy temple*. We see the truth as we note the actual word used. It is not the general word (*hieron*) that described the whole of the temple precincts, but that used for the inner shrine (*naos*). The temple in Old Testament days, and especially considered as *naos*, was above all else the special meeting-place between God and His people. It was the place on which the glory of God descended, the place of His presence. When Christ came, He made obsolete the tabernacle or temple made with hands. He Himself was the place of the divine dwelling among men, a truth that is expressed particularly in John i. 14 and ii. 19–21. That temple is no longer among men, but now God seeks as His *habitation* the lives of men who will allow Him to enter by His Spirit.

Two further points are to be noted about the apostle's thought here. First, verse 21 ends with the words *in the Lord*, and verse 22 with 'in the Spirit' (a more accurate translation than the AV *through the Spirit*), to emphasize yet again that it is only by a person being in Christ, in the Spirit (see on ii. 18), that the work of building into the habitation of God can take place. Man's abiding in Christ and Christ in man belong inextricably together (cf. Jn. xv. 4–7). None can have any true place in the eternal building of God, unless he has found life in Christ. Secondly, we are reminded how far removed the New Testament thought is from our individualistic concepts. In 1 Corinthians vi. 19 Paul does speak of the individual Christian's body as the 'temple (*naos*) of the Holy Ghost', but his thought dwells rather on the community of Christians as the temple (2 Cor. vi. 16), or as one organism indwelt by the living Christ. It is true that unity is not a matter of organization, but of the sharing of the common life and tasks of the body, but it behoves all Christians to take warning of the danger of individualistic Christian service, and to consider seriously the things that hinder the expression of that common life and the fulfilling of the tasks. In Philippians ii. 1–3 and iv. 2 Paul had to speak against divisions due to personal rivalries, and in 1 Corinthians i and iii against the danger of breaking up into sects for the sake of loyalty to persons rather than to Christ. Here he has had in mind the Jewish-Gentile animosities that in earlier days threatened to make two churches instead of one, and now to Gentile Christians he says—what many Jewish Christians before had been loth to accept—*ye also are builded together* into this *holy temple*, this *habitation of God* in *the Spirit*.

c. The privilege of proclamation (iii. 1-13)

1. There is a pattern of development in these first three chapters of the Epistle. In chapter i the apostle's meditation on the wealth of the blessings of God in Christ has led naturally to prayer. In chapter ii he has developed further his great theme of the purpose of God in Christ, as he has spoken of the amazing grace of God in bringing those dead in sin to new life in Christ, and of the far-reaching significance of the reconciling of Jew and Gentile together in the one people of God. His expression of these great facts, which have a practical importance that touches the whole of life, leads him naturally to prayer again. So he begins *For this cause* (cf. i. 15) and he is about to add 'I bow my knees' (verse 14), but deeply aware of his position and the nature of his relationship with those to whom he writes, and for whom he would pray, he says, *I Paul, the prisoner of Jesus Christ for you Gentiles*, and this leads him away from his prayer for a moment.

As we saw in the beginning (on i. 1) Paul's apostleship determined all his life, the work that he did, and the nature of his relationships with men. Paul could never fail to be conscious of it, as he wrote, and as he prayed. The repeated *I Paul* of his letters shows this (2 Cor. x. 1; Gal. v. 2; Col. i. 23; 1 Thes. ii. 18; Phm. 19). Now in particular 'he hears as it were the clink of his chain, and remembers where he is and why he is there' (Robinson). Because he was the apostle of the Gentiles, and very directly as a result of his stand for the equality of Jews and Gentiles in the people of God (see Acts xxi. 17-34,

xxii. 21–24, xxvi. 12–23), he was in prison. For the sake of the Gentiles he had been imprisoned, and even now his confinement was to their advantage (verse 13). He writes like this not because he was dispirited or disappointed. He wanted no pity and would allow no-one to be dejected because of his imprisonment. He saw it in a light which burnt out all self-pity. To outward appearances he was the prisoner of Rome, confined by the will of men. But just as his spiritual life 'in Christ' mattered far more to him than his outward circumstances and environment, so now he regarded himself as a prisoner by the will of his Master. Therefore he could gladly call himself *the prisoner of Jesus Christ* (cf. iv. 1; 2 Tim. i. 8; Phm. 1, 9); just as for every part of his life he could call himself the slave of Christ (e.g. Phil. i. 1).

2. His speaking like this led him, before he continued with his prayer, to dwell on his calling as the apostle to the Gentiles, and on what it meant to him. To him had been entrusted a special *dispensation of the grace of God* with particular reference to the Gentiles. In considering this word *dispensation* as it occurred in i. 10, we found that it meant basically either the administration of a household, or the office of the one who administered it. Paul here is thinking especially of the stewardship entrusted to him (cf. 1 Cor. iv. 1, ix. 17), though the other thought of the arrangement or purpose of God is not far away. Colossians i. 25 is a close parallel, and the thought is that also of Galatians ii. 7 where Paul says how 'the gospel of the uncircumcision' was entrusted to him as that 'of the circumcision' was to Peter.

To express this trust that he has he uses the word *grace*. *Grace* is used in its fullest and widest sense of the undeserved favour of God that brings man salvation (cf. i. 6f., ii. 5–8), and that freely adds to man all that he needs for living a Christian life (Acts xiii. 43, xiv. 26; 2 Cor. ix. 8). But Paul also uses it a number of times to express the privilege of being given a work to do for Christ, and to denote the particular task allotted in His service (cf. Eph. iv. 7; Rom. xii. 3, 6). In his own case it was the amazing favour of being called to be an apostle (Rom.

xv. 15f.; 1 Cor. iii. 10; Gal. ii. 9), and that to the Gentiles. There is yet another application of the word that is found in Acts xi. 23, and that rings through this whole section, that in the actual extension of the privileges of the gospel to the Gentiles the particular mercy of God had been shown. There is grace to the Gentiles that apostles of the gospel were sent to them, and grace to Paul that he should be their apostle; the two thoughts are intertwined in the use of the word *grace* in this section.

Paul feels it necessary, however, to press on his readers the fact that he has been entrusted with this grace and responsibility; and we have seen that this is a strong argument for the view that this letter was sent originally not to the Christians at Ephesus alone, but to a wider circle.[1] The AV *if ye have heard* does not quite convey the force of the Greek particle *eige* here. It does not so much express doubt (cf. its use in iv. 21; 2 Cor. v. 3; Gal. iii. 4; Col. i. 23) as call on them to verify what he is saying. Thus NEB is a better translation, 'for surely you have heard. . . .'. The argument concerning the destination still applies, however, as even this is hardly what he would say to a church that knew him as well as did Ephesus, but rather to those of whom some, at least, knew him only 'by reputation' (Scott).

3. If they appreciated the way that a special knowledge of the purpose of God for the Gentiles had been given to him, and of the particular part in the working out of that purpose that was entrusted to him, they would agree that *by revelation* God had *made known* to him *the mystery*. From i. 9 we have seen that 'revealing' and 'making known' go naturally with the word *mystery* when it is used in connection with the gospel. For this is the truth of God which is no longer hidden, but made plain to those who are willing to receive it. To Paul it had been a revelation in a special sense. Previously he had been a strict Jew of the exclusive party of the Pharisees, and it took a clear revelation from God to convince him. Moreover, at that time, the earlier apostles were not sufficiently clear and unequivocal

[1] See p. 17ff.

in their stand on the equality of the Gentiles in the people of God, and so from that standpoint also a revelation was necessary, as Paul shows in Galatians i, ii. Here he is concerned to tell not how the communication came to him, but rather the content of it. He has expressed this—the inclusion of the Gentiles with the Jews in the one body and household—and it is to what he has said already in this Epistle, not to some earlier letter, that he refers when he says, *as I wrote afore in few words*. What the grammarians call an epistolary aorist (cf. 1 Pet. v. 12) is better translated as in the NEB, 'I have already written a brief account of this.'

4. It has been suggested that *when ye read* could refer to the reading of the Old Testament, as supporting Paul's understanding of the purpose of God for the Gentiles. Matthew xxiv. 15 is compared to indicate that such a way of speaking could have reference to the Old Testament. But nowhere else in the New Testament is the Old so referred to without some specific mention of it. It is much more natural to take it as meaning that when they read what he has already written 'in few words' (verse 3), they will *understand* his *knowledge in the mystery of Christ*. Nor need we suppose that if this is the meaning, it shows in Paul a spirit of personal pride and boasting, or leads us to doubt the authenticity of the Epistle. We have considered this in dealing with the question of authorship in the Introduction. The point is that in this context, as repeatedly elsewhere, Paul is at pains to emphasize that all his understanding is by the gift of God, and only possible as He reveals His truth. The knowledge of the *mystery* was not a personal discovery upon which he could flatter himself. It was the gift of God by His Spirit (cf. i. 8, 9, 17, 18). He may pride himself in his knowledge, as he does in 2 Corinthians xi. 5f., but he realizes and states that it is only by God-given enlightenment that he possesses the truth. Moreover his purpose is not self-glorification but to help men recognize the word of God in his teaching, and thus accept its authority.

At this point we should look also into another difficulty felt in this section. What is the meaning of *the mystery of Christ* here?

In particular, is it defined in a way that is different from its definition in Colossians? It has been asserted that the difference is so great as to make common authorship impossible.[1] In Colossians i. 27 it is stated specifically that the mystery is 'Christ in you, the hope of glory', that is to say, the actual mystery, the wonderful truth that has been revealed, is that Christ comes to dwell now in the hearts of men, giving the hope of a future in the immediate presence of God. In verse 6 of this chapter the mystery seems to be taken equally specifically as 'that the Gentiles are . . . fellow-partakers of the promise in Christ Jesus through the gospel' (RV). Are these two incompatible in the same writer? Can they not be different aspects of the central revelation? In Colossians ii. 2 the mystery is simply 'Christ', and indeed it is possible to take the genitive as meaning that here. In this same Epistle (Eph. i. 9f.) it should be noted that Paul can speak of the mystery without any specific reference to the Gentiles; it is the purpose of God to 'gather together in one all things in Christ'. It therefore seems unnecessary to regard the meaning of the *mystery* in Ephesians and Colossians as being contradictory. It seems easier to say that Paul thought of the mystery as the great purpose of God in Christ. His mind dwelt now on one aspect of it, now on another; even in the same Epistle there are slight differences in the use of the word. Identity of authorship need not be questioned on the ground of such differences.

5. In Romans xvi. 25f. Paul speaks of the mystery (which there connotes the full gospel of Christ) as 'kept in silence through times eternal, but now . . . manifested' (RV). In Colossians i. 26, which is closely parallel to this section, he speaks of it as 'hid from ages and from generations, but now . . . made manifest to his saints'. Here he says the same thing in particular about the bringing in of the Gentiles. This is not to deny that there were glimpses of God's purpose in this matter in the Old Testament (as in such passages as the apostle quotes in Rom. xv. 9–12); but it is a truth that had not been at all fully understood that Jews and Gentiles should

[1] See pp. 23f.

actually become one people, and it certainly had not been carried into practical effect. *In other ages* it *was not made known unto the sons of men, as it is now revealed*; and we may take the force of the *as* to be 'in such a measure as' or 'with such clarity as' now.

To *apostles and prophets* (the prophets of the new order, as we have seen on ii. 20), *the Spirit* has been at pains to reveal this. (The phrase 'in the Spirit', RV, discussed on ii. 18 and 22, is repeated here.) The Acts of the Apostles records how the Spirit gave the revelation of this truth to Peter, and we have recalled the way in which Galatians tells the manner of the revelation to Paul. As we have seen[1] the phrase *holy apostles* is not to be considered strange, or a mark of pride, in that it was written by an apostle. *Holy* (*hagios*, see on i. 1) has not the connotation in the New Testament that it has in modern English; and without any vain-glory Paul repeatedly called himself an apostle.

6. Paul has spoken of the way that the Jews regarded the Gentiles (ii. 11), and indeed of the way in which they actually stood in relation to the people of God (ii. 12ff.). He himself had been a proud Pharisee, and shared the general Jewish disparagement of the Gentiles. His conversion meant a complete transformation in his thinking. He was turned to see Jesus, whom he had persecuted, as the Christ, the Son of God, and the only Saviour. His whole attitude to the Gentiles was also revolutionized in this same crisis of his experience. By revelation he came to see that Jews and Gentiles can now stand together in the people of God. They are *fellowheirs*, they share the same inheritance in the heavenly riches of God (i. 11–14; Gal. iii. 29, iv. 7). They are *of the same body*. One word (*sunsōma*) is used for this in the Greek; it is not known in Greek literature before Paul, and perhaps was coined by him to express this truth that the Gentiles are incorporated with Jews in the one Body of Christ (cf. ii. 16). They are also *partakers of his promise*—they share on equal terms with Jews the promise of life and salvation (cf. 2 Tim. i. 1), though

[1] See pp. 42f.

before the Gentiles were 'strangers from the covenants of promise' (Eph. ii. 12). All of these privileges they can share with the Jews because, in the same way as they, the Gentiles can now find their life *in Christ by the gospel*. The gospel, as it is preached and believed, is the effectual means, humanly speaking, by which men come to be in Christ. (Cf. the use of the same phrase in 1 Corinthians iv. 15.) That gospel, therefore, is the means and the only means of deep spiritual unity between men of however diverse racial, cultural or political backgrounds.

7. Because of this fact Paul cannot do other than speak exultantly of the privilege and responsibility and significance of his being made a *minister* of that gospel (cf. Gal. i. 13–16; Col. i. 23–29; 1 Tim. i. 12–16). The Greek word here (*diakonos*) is used sometimes in the New Testament of those of a particular office (Phil. i. 1; 1 Tim. iii. 8–12; and Acts vi. 2 where the verb *diakonein* is used); but it is often used more generally of one who lived and worked in the service (*diakonia*, as in iv. 12) of Christ. (See vi. 21 and 2 Cor. iii. 6, xi. 23; Col. i. 23; 1 Tim. iv. 6.) Paul gladly accepted the title of servant, but he realized his utter inadequacy in himself to fulfil the responsibility that it laid on him to communicate to others the word and good news of God (cf. 2 Cor. iii. 5, iv. 1, xii. 9f.). Only by a twofold gift from God was it possible for him to be such. He was a minister, *according to the gift of the grace of God given unto* him.

In our study of verse 2 we have seen the range of the use of this word *grace* in the New Testament and in particular in Paul's writings. He was unworthy to be a preacher of God's word, because he had been a persecutor; but the grace of God had made him all that he was, a new man in Christ (1 Cor. xv. 10). It also made him Christ's servant in the proclamation of His gospel, and in the particular work that he had of ministering it to the Gentiles. But mercy was not enough. He was also a minister *by the effectual working of his power*. The task to which he was called needed no mere human strength and patience and power of endurance. It needed the power of

God, and, as in i. 19, Paul shows that that power is given, and not just as an abstract thing, or as a force applied from afar, but as energizing strength (*energeia*) operative in his life by the Spirit's indwelling. In Colossians i. 29 he expresses this more fully when he says of his preaching work, 'I also labour, striving according to his working, which worketh in me mightily.' By the grace of God he was called and received as a servant of the gospel, and by the power of God he did all that was effective in that service.

8. Paul cannot stop with what he has said, but must dwell further on the incredible grace of God and on his personal unworthiness. He was *less than the least of all saints*. He invents a comparative of a superlative to express himself more forcefully.[1] This is no feigned humility. It is the inevitable attitude of one who was prostrated with wonder at the grace of God in Christ. Here it is not so much that he is consciously comparing himself with others; if he did so, he might speak as he does in 2 Corinthians xii. 11. Nor is it because he had specially in mind the fact that he had been a persecutor (as in 1 Cor. xv. 9; Gal. i. 13–15; 1 Tim. i. 12–14). Rather it is that the more he meditated on the blessings of God in Christ, and the infinite grace of His gifts, the more he realized that in himself there was nothing to make him deserve such mercy. He knew that he had no standing, no personal worthiness, no claim, no natural position or gifts, that he should receive the grace of reconciliation, and become a preacher of it. He was *less than the least*. The gospel was everything, *the unsearchable riches of Christ*.

We have seen already the apostle's love for terms that speak of wealth to express the blessings of Christ that infinitely transcend the world's riches (see on i. 7). Here he adds an adjective (*anexichniaston*) that speaks of something that cannot be traced out by human footprints. It is used of the works of God in Job v. 9 and ix. 10. If Paul had tried to measure and define that grace once, he had found himself like a man

---

[1] There is a double comparative (*meizoteran*) in 3 Jn. 4, and other similar double forms were used by Greek poets and later prose writers.

'tracking out the confines of a lake', and discovering that it was no lake at all 'but an arm of the ocean, and that he was confronted by the immeasurable sea'.[1] Those *unsearchable riches* were not simply the gospel, not doctrine, but Christ Himself (cf. Mt. xiii. 44). And the inestimable privilege of Paul's calling was to present Christ to the Gentiles who had not heard of Him before, nor been included in His kingdom (cf. Acts ix. 15, xxii. 21, xxvi. 17f.; Rom. xi. 13, xv. 16–21; Gal. ii. 7–9).

9. In the first place the task of the apostle was simply to make known the unsearchable riches of Christ to those who had not heard of them before. But as men came to faith in Him, the preacher's work was to go on to share the knowledge of the wonderful purpose of God. So Paul describes his task as 'bringing to light' (NEB) this great truth. The MSS here vary between including and excluding the word *pantas*, translated *all men* in AV; and accordingly we have a meaning of the verb *phōtisai* that requires or does not require a personal object. The slightly more likely position is that *all men* should be omitted, and the verb taken (as in 1 Cor. iv. 5 and 2 Tim. i. 10) to mean 'showing forth' or 'bringing to light' God's truth. The word is in fact 'the natural word to use for the public disclosure of what had been kept secret' (Robinson).

There are two further textual difficulties in this verse. The AV reading *fellowship* translates *koinōnia*, which we now know to be the reading of only a few, less important, MSS, and the weight of evidence supports *oikonomia*, 'dispensation' (RV) as the original reading. In other words, we have again the term that was used in iii. 2 (as in i. 10), and here its meaning must be God's 'plan' (RSV) or 'purpose' (NEB). Paul is thus expressing again the fact that his work is to show and teach the great purpose of God in Christ. It is a *mystery* (as he has said in verses 4, 5) not at all fully communicated to men before, but by no means an after-thought in the mind of God. God is spoken of here as the One *who created all things*, in order to imply that this was His purpose from the beginning of the creation,

[1] J. H. Jowett, *The Passion for Souls*, p. 10.

though in His wisdom He chose to reveal it to man in stages. Here at the end of the verse we have the third textual variant. The words *by Jesus Christ* are not in the best MSS, and probably they were added as a comment, true in itself, but such as turns the mind from the main point here, which is not that Christ was Agent in creation, but that this purpose of God reaches back into the past as far as does His creative work.

10. What was hinted at in ii. 7 now is expressed specifically. This great purpose of God for the Church reaches out beyond this world order and beyond the present time. It has to be declared now to all men, but the hosts of heaven also, who know the glory of God's creation, are through the Church to be enlightened concerning His work for man's salvation. Spiritual beings, *the principalities and powers in heavenly places*, as we have seen on i. 21, were given a prominent place in the early Gnostic systems that were being developed at this time. Paul, in accepting the existence of such beings, not only insists that all were made by Christ and are subject to Him, but also shows that in one way at least human beings in the blood-bought Church of God have a superior position to them all. They know and are to declare to these spiritual powers (cf. 1 Pet. i. 12) the redeeming purpose and work of the Almighty, the aspects of *the manifold wisdom of God* that otherwise they cannot know. Here, as in verse 8, a descriptive adjective is used that is pregnant with meaning. It is *polupoikilos* (the simple form *poikilos* is used in 1 Pet. iv. 10), a word that means variegated, and that was used in classical Greek writers with reference to cloth or flowers, and so here it suggests 'the intricate beauty of an embroidered pattern' (Robinson) or the endless variety of colours in flowers. Such, the apostle says, is the wisdom of God that the Church declares.

11. The connection of this verse with what has gone before is probably not so much that the declaration to the angels is of the eternal purpose, but that the wisdom of God is concerned with *the eternal purpose which he purposed in Christ Jesus our Lord*. We are back again to this great, central theme of the

Epistle. Behind all the events of this world's history there is an eternal purpose being worked out. God's is no *ad hoc* plan, but one conceived from eternity and eternal in its scope. Christ is the Agent of this purpose. The verb here would be literally rendered as the purpose which God 'made' or 'did'. By some it is understood as the purpose which God 'achieved' (NEB) or 'wrought out' in Christ. It seems more likely that it is the purpose *which he purposed*, as AV takes it, though the Greek is not quite the usual form of expression for this. The difference in meaning is not great, as this Epistle shows that the beginning and the fruition of the purpose is in Him, and the emphasis on His work is borne out by the fullness of His name in this context, which we might translate, 'the Christ, even Jesus our Lord'. Each name, that which speaks of the preparation for His coming, that which refers to His incarnate life, and that which shows His position in the whole universe, adds to our understanding of His work.

12. Now from the exalted, cosmic view, the apostle turns to the most practical significance that it has for the everyday life of the Christian. To this mighty God, whose purpose embraces heaven and earth, time and eternity, *we, in* Christ, *have boldness and access with confidence*. The word *boldness* (*parrēsia*) is basically 'freedom of speech'. It is often used of boldness before men, as in vi. 20, Acts iv. 31 and Philippians i. 20, the absence of fear or shame. It is used of a similar absence of fear or shame in approaching God. Hebrews iv. 16 and x. 19 are the clearest examples and explanations of this, which is the meaning here. Linked with this word is that which has been used already in ii. 18, here translated *access*; and in the light of the following phrases it is clear that it is again the intransitive use of the word that is right. *Access with confidence* expresses a thought very similar to that of boldness, but it is more personal. Faith in Him is the means of access (cf. Rom. v. 1f.). The forgiveness of sins that makes access possible is the gift of God's grace received on man's side by faith (Eph. ii. 8f.), faith which regularly in the Pauline Epistles means no mere intellectual belief, but personal knowledge of and attachment to Christ.

13. Because of that freedom of approach to the eternal Lord Himself, and because of the greatness of His purpose within the scope and glory of which every Christian has been brought, Paul urges that there should be no faintheartedness in the face of his tribulations. The difference between translations here indicates an ambiguity in the Greek which can be taken in three different ways. As no subject of the second verb is expressed, it could be 'I ask that I may not faint. . . .', but in the context this is the least likely. It could be a prayer, as RV can be understood, 'I ask that ye faint not', but this verb *aitoumai* is not normally understood as meaning 'pray' unless the name of God is mentioned as the One to whom the request is made. It is more likely, as AV and NEB clearly make it, that we have an entreaty addressed to the readers, *I desire that ye faint not at my tribulations.* Paul was aware of the fact that they were tempted to lose heart because he, the apostle and champion of the Gentiles, was in prison. (See on vi. 21f.) This they must not do, but rather realize that his sufferings were their gain and *glory.* It was true that he was suffering imprisonment *for* them, because he had given his life to preach the gospel to the Gentiles, and because he had stood for the equality of Gentiles with Jews in the one people of God (see on iii. 1). But in his willingness to do this, and in the grace of Christ given to him in imprisonment, they could glory. Their apostle was continuing to live out and show forth the sufferings of Christ (Col. i. 24), and because this was all in the loving wisdom and purpose of God, they could be sure that Christ was being magnified by Paul's weakness and confinement even more than He would be by a continuous successful mission. (Cf. 2 Cor. iv. 7–12, xii. 9–12; Phil. i. 12ff.)

d. Renewed prayer (iii. 14–21)

14. Now Paul takes up again the words with which he began in iii. 1, *for this cause,* and this time he utters his prayer. It has an added force now in the light of what he has just said. Not only is he led to prayer by the thought of the greatness of the grace of Christ raising to life those who were dead in sin, and by the realization of the unity into which Jew and Gentile have been brought in the one household, but also by the contemplation of the whole wonderful purpose of God which he has been led now to express more deeply and more personally. In the light of these things and, we have to add, the temptation of his readers to lose heart, he prays now as he does. It is a prayer like that of i. 15ff., but it has an even greater intensity, as is implied in the words *I bow my knees unto the Father*. Among the Jews it was usual to stand to pray (see Matthew vi. 5 and Luke xviii. 11, 13). Kneeling for prayer, though it has become a regular Christian attitude, was formerly an expression of deep emotion or earnestness, and on that basis we must understand Paul's words here. Solomon knelt at the dedication of the temple (1 Ki. viii. 54); Stephen at the time of his martyrdom (Acts vii. 60); Peter at the death-bed of Dorcas (Acts ix. 40); Paul at the time of his farewells on his last journey to Jerusalem (Acts xx. 36, xxi. 5); our Lord Himself in His agony in Gethsemane (Lk. xxii. 41).

15. At the end of verse 14, following the best MSS, we should omit the words *of our Lord Jesus Christ* (so RV and NEB) but as is so often the case, the name of the One to whom Paul prays is qualified to bring out the depth of the meaning and significance of his prayer (cf. i. 17). God is not only Father, but He is also the One from whom alone all the fatherhood that there is derives its meaning and inspiration. This verse has been variously translated. The Greek words *pasa patria* cannot be taken as *the whole family*—the article would be required for this. The meaning therefore is not simply that all in heaven and earth have Him as Father. RV and NEB 'every family' is closer. The word cannot quite be translated 'fatherhood' (RV mg.). It means strictly 'lineage' or 'pedigree' (on the father's side) or more often a 'tribe' or even 'nation', but by the context and the derivation of the word ('father' is *patēr* in the Greek), the idea of fatherhood is there. In effect the apostle is saying, think of any 'father-headed group' (Allan) *in heaven and earth*. Each one is named from Him. From Him it derives its existence and its concept and experience of fatherhood. As Severian (quoted by Robinson) puts it, 'The name of father did not go up from us, but from above it came to us.' To such a Father, Father of all, the One in whom alone fatherhood is seen in perfection, men come when they come to pray.

This qualification, like that of i. 17, gives strength to prayer. With it we may compare the Lord's specific comparison between human fatherhood and the divine fatherhood in Matthew vii. 11 in the matter of giving 'good things to them that ask'. We may note also the use that the apostle makes of human relationships to teach divine truth. Our knowledge of God is helped by the suggestion that all that we know of human fatherhood at its best is true, but to an infinitely higher degree, of God in His relation to us. At the same time the concept of human fatherhood is infinitely ennobled by the comparison. Exactly the same is true of the apostle's treatment of the husband-wife relationship in v. 22–33.

16. The qualification of the name 'Father' has been added to strengthen faith for prayer. The reminder of his resources now has the same purpose. Yet again this Epistle speaks of *the riches* of God (see on i. 7), and the preposition is significant. Paul does not pray merely that God will give 'out of the treasures of his glory' (NEB), but *according to* them (cf. Phil. iv. 19). He gives without limit because He Himself is infinitely greater than 'the measure of man's mind'; and the riches that He gives are of His very nature (see on 'glory' in i. 6).

The first gift for which prayer is made here is strength. So it was in i. 19, and, as there, this power of God is not expressed by just a single word (cf. also vi. 10 and Col. i. 11). That they may be *strengthened with might*, the apostle prays. The verb *krataiōthēnai* speaks of being made strong or capable. A person can be made strong in love or knowledge or some other quality; at this point the prayer is that Paul's readers may be equipped with the power (*dunamis*) that makes them able to stand firm in Christ, and to live and work for Him (cf. 1 Cor. xvi. 13; Phil. iv. 13). This prayer, however, speaks further of the means and the sphere of operation of this power. It is the constant assumption, or specific emphasis, of the teaching of the New

Testament, that strength for the Christian life comes by the personal indwelling of the Holy Spirit. In 2 Corinthians iv. 16 this phrase is used in distinction from what is external, as Paul says 'though our outward man perish, yet the inward man is renewed day by day'. It may include, or at least it affects, all that the New Testament means when it speaks of heart, mind, will and spirit. It is the deep seat of the personality, where the Spirit seeks to have His dwelling and so transform the whole life of a man.

17, 18. Another way of expressing the work that it is God's purpose to do in man, and which therefore can be an object of prayer on behalf of others, is *that Christ may dwell in* their *hearts.* The indwelling of Christ in the heart, and the strengthening by the Spirit coming into the inner man, are not two different experiences. Paul is not always precise in distinguishing the work of Christ and of the Spirit in man, as Romans viii. 9f. well shows (cf. Jn. xiv. 16–18). If he were using strict theological terminology he might speak simply of the Spirit in such a context. But such is the unity of the Christ preached to them, and Him who indwells, that sometimes he prefers to speak as he does in this verse. The verb he uses (*katoikein*) is also significant, for it is in contrast to one that speaks of a transitory dwelling in a place (*paroikein*, from which we have the noun used in ii. 19). The thought is precisely that of the hymn, 'Come not to sojourn, but abide with me'. Then once again *faith* is described as the requirement on man's side, the attitude that receives Him. The Christ waits only for this willingness and desire that He should come in with all the fullness of blessing that His presence conveys (cf. Rev. iii. 20).

His presence means not only strength, but wisdom, inspiration, and above all love; and it is to love that the prayer now turns, and love continues as its theme to the end. Grammatically the second half of verse 17 is connected with verse 18. It is possible to take the words *in love* with the first half of the verse (as in NEB). They stand before the participles, and it is true that several times in this Epistle the words bring a clause to an emphatic close (i. 4, iv. 2, 16). Yet the phrase would seem in this case rather to overload the preceding clause, and appears to be needed with the participles. So it seems better to understand the prayer as for the indwelling of Christ by faith, and then for such a firm establishing of their lives in love, that they may go on to a deep understanding of God. It is thus preferable to take the whole of the participial phrase as within the clause of verse 18 (as do AV and RV). There is no difficulty in the mixing of the metaphors of these two participles (cf. Col. ii. 17 and the similar combination in 1 Cor. iii. 9). Both are often used by the apostle. The roots of Christian character are to go down deeply, and its foundation is to be firmly laid, and love is the means of both.

Paul was aware of a danger, especially in the churches of the Greek world, of a faith that depended simply on intellectual knowledge (cf. 1 Cor. i. 22; Col. ii. 18, 23; 1 Tim. i. 4, vi. 4). He is not so much arguing against an approach to faith in Christ which is barren because it is merely intellectual, as clearly showing again and again that his own line of approach is totally different. He realized that 'true knowledge', the knowledge of God, 'is unattainable without love' (Scott). If there is no love, the Spirit of Christ is not present, and there can be no understanding. John vii. 17 and xv. 9ff. express this same fact by showing that understanding comes where there is obedience, which is the fruit of love. The impossibility of holding the faith of Christ without love is one of the great themes of 1 John. In fact these verses give two reasons why understanding proceeds of necessity from love.

In the first place, the truth is not apprehended by an individual in isolation but *with all the saints*; and secondly, the content of the knowledge and wisdom of God is love. Chapter iv. 7ff. will indicate that the individual members of Christ's Body can grow in understanding and in strength only as each possesses and uses for the benefit of all the varying gifts of the Spirit, gifts that make them able to work as apostles, prophets, evangelists, pastors and teachers, 'for the edifying of the body'. It is also true that men are limited in the very understanding of the purpose of God until they see it working out, and they themselves are parts of its outworking, in the 'fellowship of the saints'. The word translated *may be able* (RV and NEB 'may be strong'—Gk. *exischusēte*) and also the verb *apprehend* (*katalabesthai*), meaning an earnest grasping, suggest the difficulty of the task envisaged, simply because it is no mere intellectual feat, but a matter of practical experience, a living together in love which is no easy thing. We are not intended to give detailed meanings to *the breadth, and length, and depth, and height*; rather we are to feel with heart and mind and intuition the 'many dimensions' of love, and work to weave that love into all the fabric of life.

19. Nevertheless the definite goal to which the Christian life must move, and for which therefore the apostle prays, is for his readers *to know the love of Christ*, to know how He loved and loves, and to experience His love in loving Him and loving others for His sake. Yet even here Paul cannot escape the paradox. In the Greek between the verb and its object there is this qualification that apparently contradicts the verb—the love *passeth knowledge* (cf. Phil. iv. 7). The love of Christ is infinitely greater than man can fully know or imagine, and it is also much more than any object of knowledge; it is superior to knowledge (1 Cor. viii. 1), even to spiritual knowledge (1 Cor. xiii. 2). It must find expression in experience, in sorrows and joys, trials and sufferings, in ways too deep for the mind of man to fathom, or for human language to express.

The climax of the apostle's prayer for his fellow-Christians is that they *might be filled with all the fulness of God*. He prays that they may receive not any attribute of God, or any gift of His, not love, not knowledge, not strength, alone or in combination—but no less than the very highest he can pray for, the full indwelling of God. Those who speak of the impossibility of this are in danger of missing the point. Of course the eternal God can never be limited to the capacity of any one, or all, of His sinful creatures; but the apostle does not want to pray for anything less than that God's people may be filled to (*eis*) the very fullest of Himself that He seeks to bring into their lives (see on i. 23). For his own life, and for those to whom he ministers, Paul wants no less than the Spirit's full indwelling (v. 18). Of His fullness, and not just of a part of His nature, all may receive (Jn. i. 16); and the goal for the individual and for the Body must be nothing short of 'the measure of the stature of the fulness of Christ' (iv. 13).

20. Robinson well says, 'No prayer that has ever been framed has uttered a bolder request.' Yet 'unabashed by the greatness of his petition, he triumphantly invokes a power which can do far more than he asks, far more than even his lofty imagination conceives.' Often with Paul intercession takes up from praise, and here it also leads to praise because of the thought of the greatness that is the Lord's and the magnitude of the gifts that he knows he has been able to ask of Him in faith. He is *able to do exceeding abundantly above all that we ask or think.* Other New Testament doxologies speak thus of His infinite ability (e.g. Rom. xvi. 25 and Jude 24). There is no limit to His power; only man's words and thoughts about it are limited. This power, moreover, Paul will repeat, is the power *according to* which (see on verse 16) God acts, and that not as an external force, but as that which *worketh in us*. It is present in men's lives when Christ is indwelling (verse 17), and when the Holy Spirit is operative in the inward man (verse 16), energizing them there (*energoumai*—see on i. 19).

21. In the manner of most doxologies Paul says that to God glory is due through all eternity—'to all generations, for ever and ever' (RSV). If we are to analyse such an expression, its implication is that His praise is to go on to all generations to the consummation of time in eternity. The distinctive feature of this doxology lies in the two ways in which that glory is said to be shown and the praise declared. First, it is *in the church*. The Church is the sphere of the outworking of God's purpose on earth, and even in heaven it will have the task of proclaiming the manifold wisdom of God (iii. 10). It is never to take glory to itself (cf. Ps. cxv. 1); its goal is to give praise and glory to Him (i. 6, 12, 14). Then secondly, it is *in Christ Jesus* Himself, for it is God's purpose 'in Christ'—Christ the Beginning, Christ the Saviour, Christ the Source of unity—that has been the apostle's theme in these chapters. This is the goal of Paul's vision that inspires all his work. 'God is all in all. At this furthest horizon of thought, Christ and His own are seen together rendering to God unceasing glory' (Findlay). They are coupled in the infinitely wonderful purpose of God—perhaps already there is a hint of the imagery of chapter v and of Revelation xxi—Bride and Bridegroom, redeemed and Redeemer. The glory of God is most gloriously seen in the grace of His uniting His sinful creatures to His eternal, sinless Son.

III. UNITY IN THE BODY OF CHRIST (iv. 1-16)

a. Maintaining the unity (iv. 1-6)

1. As is often the case in Paul's Epistles, the doxology marks the end of a section. The doxology at the end of chapter iii marks the close of the part of the Epistle that is predominantly doctrinal. Chapters iv–vi are to show in practical detail how glory is to be rendered to God now in the Church (iii. 21). The apostle begins here as he did in chapter iii, by referring to himself as a *prisoner* (see on iii. 1), but this time 'the prisoner in the Lord' (RV) is the true reading. The chains of his imprisonment limited his bodily movement, but his life was most truly controlled by the fact that it was 'in the Lord'. The fact that his life in and for Christ had led to imprisonment did not mean that he requested the sympathy of his readers, but it added intensity to his appeal, as now he wished to speak to them concerning the whole manner of their life. He has set before them the great purpose of God in Christ for His Church. He has prayed that they may know the wonder of His plan, His love, His power, and every spiritual blessing that He offers. But now in these remaining chapters he is going to write about the quality and kind of life that is demanded of them individually and in the fellowship of Christ's Church.

It is no mere *teaching* of the Christian ethic that the apostle seeks to give. He whose greatest concern in life has become to 'present every man perfect in Christ Jesus' (Col. i. 28—cf. Acts xx. 27, 31) makes earnest entreaty. The word *parakalō* can mean 'exhort', but obviously in this context has its stronger meaning *beseech* (cf. 2 Cor. v. 20). The link with what precedes is given by the word *therefore* as in Romans xii. 1, indicating that Christian conduct follows from Christian doctrine, that the Christian's duty derives directly from the unspeakable debt of gratitude that he owes for all that he has received in Christ. In the most general terms, that duty is that they should *walk worthy* of their *vocation*. We are back to three great Pauline words (cf. 1 Thes. ii. 12). Step by step they are to walk (see on ii. 2) in a direction that corresponds to their call (i. 18). That call to know the grace of God in Christ, to be the children of God, and to serve Him as His 'dedicated ones' and messengers of His gospel, should transform every part of life. For it involves the obligation to live in a manner that is in accordance with the name of Him whose they are and whom they serve (Phil. i. 29), pleasing Him in all things (Col. i. 10). 'Those who have been chosen by God to sit with Christ in the heavenly places must remember that the honour of Christ is involved in their daily lives.' So Bruce comments, adding that this first far-reaching instruction is 'a principle to guide in every situation'.

2. Four particular aspects of such a life are now named, and they are more than personal qualities. For the life worthy of the calling of God is a life in the fellowship of the people of God; and if this is to be maintained these four virtues are vital. The first, emphasized by the characteristic *all* (cf. i. 8, iv. 19, 31, v. 3, 9, vi. 18), is *lowliness*. Very significantly, the Greek noun *tapeinophrosunē* does not seem to have been used before New Testament times, and the corresponding adjective *tapeinos* nearly always had a bad meaning, and was associated with words with the sense of slavish, mean, ignoble. Lessons of humility had been taught in the Old Testament, and such a passage as Isaiah lxvi. 2 in the LXX is a notable exception to the general pre-Christian use of *tapeinos*, but to the Greeks humility was not a virtue. To them, as indeed to most non-Christian peoples in any generation, the concept of 'the fulness of life . . . left no room for humility' (Robinson). In Christ lowliness became a virtue. His life and death were service and sacrifice without thought of reputation (Phil. ii. 6f.). Because the Christian is called to follow in His steps, humility has an irreplaceable part in the Christian character (cf. Acts xx. 19), and also for the reason that he has been brought to see the greatness and glory and holiness of God, so that he cannot but be overwhelmed by the realization of his own weakness and sinfulness.

The second word, *meekness* (*prautēs*), was used in classical Greek in the good sense of mildness or gentleness of character. The adjective (*praos*), especially, found an important use in describing an animal completely disciplined and controlled. *Meekness* in the New Testament is used of a person's attitude to the word of God (Jas. i. 21), but more often of his attitude to other people (1 Cor. iv. 21; 2 Tim. ii. 25; Tit. iii. 2). It is closely connected with the spirit of submissiveness which becomes the keynote of this Epistle when in v. 21 the apostle turns to speak of human relationships. The man who is meek does not assert his own importance or authority (the word is very aptly used in Nu. xii. 3 to describe the character of Moses); he has 'every instinct and every passion, every motion of his mind and heart and tongue and desire, under perfect control' (Barclay)—the control of God.

Thirdly, there is *longsuffering* (*makrothumia*), a word sometimes used of steadfast endurance of suffering or misfortune (as in Jas. v. 10), but more often, as is the case here, of slowness in avenging wrong or retaliating when hurt by another. It is used of God's patience with men (Rom. ii. 4, ix. 22; 1 Tim. i. 16; 1 Pet. iii. 20; 2 Pet. iii. 15), and the corresponding and consequent quality that the Christian should show towards others (1 Cor. xiii. 4; Gal. v. 22; Col. iii. 12; 2 Tim. iv. 2).

Forbearance, the fourth requirement, is also a divine quality (Rom. ii. 4). It is the practical outworking of longsuffering. 'It involves bearing with one another's weaknesses, not ceasing to love one's neighbours or friends because of those faults in them which perhaps offend or displease us' (Abbott). Such forbearance, and indeed all these four qualities, are possible only *in love*. For love is the basic attitude of seeking the highest good of others, and it will therefore lead to all these qualities, and include them all (see verses 15, 16 and on i. 4). Paul has prayed that his readers may be 'rooted and grounded in love' (iii. 17), and now he exhorts them to do their part, and to go on to possess all these virtues *in love*.

3. All that now follows in the rest of the letter may be considered as an expansion of the appeal that has just been made. But its first particular application is to the unity of Christians. Some have taken *the unity of the Spirit* here to mean the spiritual unity of the Church in the sense that human spirits are linked together wherever men and women are found sharing the things that they have 'in Christ'. We have noted already (on i. 17) that it is sometimes difficult to tell exactly how we should translate and interpret this word 'spirit'. Here, however, it is almost certain that the apostle views the unity as the gift of God. It was made possible by the cross of Christ (ii. 14ff.), and is made effective by the working *of the Spirit* of God. It cannot be created by man; it is given to him, but his responsibility is to *keep* it, to guard it in the face of many attempts from within and without the Church to take it away. The translation *endeavouring* is not strong enough to do justice to the Greek word *spoudazontes*. It suggests the legitimate possibility of failure, whereas the Greek word conveys rather the idea of zealous effort and care (cf. 1 Thes. ii. 17; 2 Tim. ii. 15; 2 Pet. i. 10, 15, iii. 14). RV 'giving diligence', or NEB 'spare no effort' are preferable renderings.

But, as with his practical bent the apostle has in the previous verse added forbearance to longsuffering, so here to the abstract 'oneness' (a word which in fact he hardly ever uses) he adds the means to such unity, which is maintained by keeping *the bond of peace*. If by love (which the parallel passage in Col. iii. 14 calls 'the bond of perfectness') men can live in the peace that Christ has brought them, then unity will be kept indeed.

4. The apostle is aware of the endless variety of temperaments amongst his readers and the diverse racial and social backgrounds from which they have come into the Christian

Church; but he would have them even more aware of the spiritual realities that now unite them and that should completely transcend differences of background. Already, in i. 13, 14 he has spoken of the spiritual blessings that are now shared between Jews and Gentiles, and in ii. 11–22 of the barriers between them that have been broken down in Christ. All, he says, now have equal shares in the privileges of grace (iii. 6). Here, as in a credal summary, perhaps a fragment of an early Christian hymn (see on v. 19), he names what they have in common, a unity by the Spirit in the Church, a unity in Christ acknowledged and confessed as Lord, a unity ultimately in God the Father and Source of all.

They are brought to be *one body*. To be 'in Christ' means to be in His Body (see on i. 1), members one of another as truly and intimately as are the organs of the human body. The unity is indeed a spiritual unity, and therefore transcends and surpasses any association or society with its basis in the things of this world. Yet we must beware of thinking of it simply as spiritual and unseen. To say 'one body' is more than to say that people are of 'one spirit'. The sense of spiritual kinship did not satisfy Paul. The apostle who was so concerned with the practical unity of Jews and Gentiles in the Church, and with the working together of all Christians, would surely have abhorred many of the divisions that we accept. Where differences in essential doctrine and contradictions in ethical teaching make such divisions, he would strive to know and uphold the way of Christ in each detail. Where differences are caused merely by superficial things or by the selfish individualism of members, he would toil and fight for the breaking down of barriers and the working out of genuine fellowship. It was right and necessary for the Reformers to uphold the doctrine of the 'invisible Church' as against a view that membership of an outward organization meant *ipso facto* membership of Christ; but at the same time the New Testament shows that in the sight of God there is *one body* of Christ, and in loyalty to Him Christians are impelled to strive to 'let the relations of practical Christian life and work correspond to that fact, to the utmost possible' (Moule, *CB*).

There is also *one Spirit*, and the AV is surely right in taking it as the Holy Spirit. The following verses refer to the Father and the Son,[1] and we have a close parallel to ii. 18 which has spoken of our 'access by one Spirit unto the Father' (cf. 1 Cor. xii. 13). All who are members of the one body are that by virtue of the one Spirit of God dwelling in them (Rom. viii. 9). This fact prevents any view of the Church as a mere organization; for the presence of the Spirit constitutes the Church, and is the basis of its unity. Then, all who have the Spirit have a common *hope*. From a vast variety of backgrounds they have come, but their goal is now the same. The Spirit is the earnest (i. 14) and the pledge that in the end all will stand together in the presence of the Lord and be restored fully to His likeness and possess His inheritance. For those who share the glory of that hope (i. 18; Rom. v. 2; Col. i. 27), and are concerned to give witness of it to the world, it is folly not to strive now to keep a unity in peace and love.

5. There is also *one Lord*, even Jesus Christ. This, as 1 Corinthians xii. 3 shows us, was the basic, primitive Christian creed (cf. 1 Cor. viii. 6; Phil. ii. 11). It expresses more, however, than a belief that is shared; it speaks of a common allegiance to *one* transcendent *Lord*, and where this is more than mere lip-service (cf. Mt. vii. 21), it should bind men together more than anything else. Where there is 'the same Lord' (Rom. x. 12), Jews and Gentiles, black and white, rich and poor, great and small, are yoked together. Neither personal ambition, nor party spirit, nor disputes about non-essentials will be allowed to break such unity, if Christ is served and honoured as Lord.

It is possible that the *one faith* means the same attitude of trust that binds all to the Lord, the same way of access to Him and means of life in Him. Or it may be that here, and then in verse 13, it means the same vital truths concerning Him and His work and purpose. This way of speaking of 'the faith' was

---

[1] Verses 4-6 here, like 1 Cor. xii. 4-6, are verses in which the doctrine of the Trinity is implicit. Though the word Trinity is never used, in such passages the naming together of Father, Son and Holy Spirit and their divine functions makes the doctrine inescapable. Cf. Mt. xxviii. 19; 2 Cor. xiii. 14.

indeed more common later (1 Tim. iii. 9, iv. 1, 6; Tit. i. 4; Jude 3), but it seems to be used in much this sense in Galatians i. 23 and also in Philippians i. 25 and Colossians ii. 7.

The outward sign of this faith (whichever way we take it), and the 'visible word' expressing the work of Christ was *baptism.* Instituted by the Lord Himself, it was an experience that every Christian shared. All had passed through the same initiation. All had been 'baptized into Christ' (Gal. iii. 27), not into a variety of leaders, as Paul, Peter and Apollos (1 Cor. i. 13), nor into a plurality of churches. 'By one Spirit', Paul says in 1 Corinthians xii. 13, 'are we all baptized into one body.' The sacrament is therefore a sacrament of unity. It is often asked why no reference was made here to the other great sacrament of the gospel, expressing as it did, even more obviously, the unity and the sharing that there should be between all Christians. Perhaps it is that an argument such as that in 1 Corinthians x. 16f. would be needed to demonstrate this, rather than just a single word; or perhaps, as Westcott suggests, 'the Apostle is speaking of the initial conditions of Christian life', whereas 'Holy Communion belongs to the support and development of it'.

6. Ultimately the unity is in the *one God and Father of all* (cf. 1 Cor. viii. 6, xii. 5, 6). All are His creatures, made in His image as His sons from the beginning, and through Christ brought back as His children (see on i. 5). Therefore all Christians are of one and the same family, and share the conviction that God is their Father, and *above all, and through all, and in . . . all* (cf. Rom. xi. 36). Whether in a world with deities for each city or nation or aspect of life, as the world of Paul's day, or in a world which to all practical purposes has renounced God, such conviction about Him should bind men more closely than any human tie. Christians believe that they 'live in a God-created, God-controlled, God-sustained, God-filled world' (Barclay), and even more, that God indwells them and is working out His purpose through them. Where can such depth and breadth of unity be found as in the fellowship of those who share this faith and experience? It follows inevitably that unnecessary divisions are folly, and weaken the Church's witness in the world to such a glorious faith.

b. Diversity in unity (iv. 7–16)

7. The great heritage of the faith all Christians share, and having this in common they are responsible to guard the unity of the Spirit. But they may not expect their personalities, their gifts and their tasks to be all alike. In His wisdom, and to make each dependent on others, God has ordained not uniformity but an endless variety of gifts for the members of the body. As Calvin puts it, 'no member of the body of Christ is endowed with such perfection as to be able, without the assistance of others, to supply his own necessities.' *Unto every one of us is given* different gifts for the benefit of all. Paul uses the word *grace* here in the sense in which we have found it used in iii. 2, 7, 8: the privilege of a special calling in the service of God. The word implies that there is no place for boasting; none has anything other than what he has received unmerited (cf. 1 Cor. iv. 7). No-one has all the gifts; and also it is true that no member of the body is without some spiritual task and spiritual gift for it. To each—not ministers or leaders alone— such grace is given *according to the measure of the gift of Christ*. These words suggest the Lord's portioning out, in His wisdom, different kinds of gifts to different members. Both the words *measure* and *grace* are used with the meaning they have here in Romans xii. 3–8, and 1 Corinthians xii. 4 has the same thought as this when it says that 'there are diversities of gifts, but the same Spirit'.

8. At this point Paul leads on to a new thought. 'The measure of the gift of Christ' is that of the ascended Lord who in the days of His flesh promised such abundant bestowal when He returned to the Father's presence (Jn. xiv. 12–14). To express this the apostle quotes Scripture, Psalm lxviii. 18, a passage which significantly enough was associated with Pentecost in the synagogue lectionary (Bruce), and which could be applied to the triumph and ascension of the Lord, followed by the bestowal of spiritual gifts to His Church. In their original setting the words of the Psalm picture the Lord returning in triumph (either to the Jerusalem sanctuary, or to heaven itself), after the overthrow of Israel's enemies. He has made His enemies captive, and they follow, as it were, in His triumphal procession. As Conqueror He has received gifts that He can bestow. Like many of the Psalms, this found ready application to the Christ. He has conquered His enemies, and returned to His Father's throne in triumph, now to bestow blessings on His people. In fact His erstwhile foes, whom He leads in 'triumph in Christ' (2 Cor. ii. 14, RV, RSV, NEB), like Paul himself, are His gifts to His Church.

We must note, however, an important change in the words used. The Hebrew Psalm has words which must be translated 'Thou hast received gifts among men.' Paul says He *gave gifts unto men.* Attempts have been made, rather unsuccessfully, to reconcile the two different wordings. Calvin, and many others, have not tried to reconcile, but think that Paul changed the words. He began by quoting the Psalm for its words that truly apply to the triumph and exaltation of Jesus, and then altered it to express the giving rather than the receiving of gifts, in accordance with the truth expressed in such a passage as Acts ii. 33. The change may have been made before Paul. Indeed the fact that the reference to the bestowal of gifts seems the main reason for the quotation makes this very probable. Perhaps in Jewish interpreters before Paul,[1] perhaps in an early Christian hymn, Paul already had the words he quoted in this form. In any case the Psalm helped him to tell that the ascension of Christ made possible the outpouring of the Spirit (Jn. vii. 39), and so these varied gifts of which he is about to speak in detail.

9, 10. We have a further difficulty to deal with in these

---

[1] The Targum on the Psalms, that may involve an interpretation going back into pre-Christian times, has 'Thou ascendedst up to the firmament, O prophet Moses, thou tookest captives captive, thou didst teach the words of the law, thou gavest them as gifts to the children of men'. The Peshitto Syriac of the Psalms has 'give' for 'receive', but this may be dependent on Paul (Robinson).

verses. When we read that *he ascended*, the meaning is clear. After His resurrection, He was exalted in glory, a fact that has been emphasized already in i. 20f. and ii. 6. And when Paul says *above all heavens*, he uses language that agrees with the Jewish definition of seven heavens, though he is not necessarily limiting himself to a spatial concept (see on i. 20). He means that Christ has been exalted to the highest honour and glory possible (Phil. ii. 9–11); He has returned to the Father from whom He came into the world. But what is the meaning of His descent? The word *first* in the AV in verse 9 is not found in the majority of the oldest MSS and it would seem that with the more recent English versions we should omit the word as a later interpretative addition to the text. Some have taken it to be an addition by mistaken interpretation, and that the descent was that which Christ made by His Spirit after Pentecost. Strongly against this is the association of the giving of the gifts to men with His ascension rather than His descent (in verse 8). So we may permit *first*, though not original, to interpret the meaning for us, and allow the tense in RSV, 'he had also descended into the lower parts of the earth.'

What then did the apostle mean by *the lower parts of the earth*? Some have been led by these words to set this passage alongside 1 Peter iii. 19 and iv. 6, understood as referring to a descent of Christ after His crucifixion to preach the gospel to those who had died before His coming. The exact meaning of the 1 Peter passages is not certain, but whatever their meaning, there seems no reason to suppose that there is this kind of reference here to His preaching to the dead. Above the highest heaven He ascended, and He had been to the deepest depths of earth. This may mean simply this earth, so low in comparison with His heavenly home (cf. Is. xliv. 23); or it may denote the fact that He suffered the greatest humiliation when He endured death itself (cf. Phil. ii. 8), and thus descended to what Scripture sometimes calls 'the depths of the earth' (cf. Ps. lxix. 15; Rom. x. 7).

There seem to be two points that the apostle is wanting to stress here. First, it is Christ's will and purpose for everything to be pervaded with His presence (cf. i. 10). He has descended and ascended *that he might fill all things*. He is supreme over all the powers both of heaven and earth (cf. Col. i. 16ff.); there is nothing that is not subject to Him, no place or order of existence where His presence may not be known and felt. Both the descent and the ascent have this purpose. In particular, as Barclay puts it, 'the ascension of Jesus meant not a Christ-deserted, but a Christ-filled world' because of the giving of His Spirit (cf. Jn. xvi. 7). Secondly, we are to realize that the ascended Lord whom the Church now worships is the same as He who came down and lived among men, sharing their sorrows, trials and temptations, and therefore that He feels those of His people today.

11. Now Paul goes on to speak of the specific gifts that He has given to men. In the light of verses 7, 8 we must not take *gave* as merely equivalent to 'appointed'. All, in their particular ministries, are God's gift to the Church. 'To Christ', says Calvin, 'we owe it that we have ministers of the gospel.' The Church may appoint men to different work and functions, but unless they have the gifts of the Spirit, and therefore are themselves the gifts of Christ to His Church, their appointment is valueless. The expression also 'serves well to remind ministers that the gifts of the Spirit are not for the enrichment of oneself but for the enrichment of the Church' (Allan).

At the later date which some would give to this Epistle it would seem almost impossible not to have reference to the local ministry of bishops, presbyters and deacons which had come to be of greatest importance to the Church. As it is, the apostle is not thinking of the ministers of Christ in their *offices*, but rather according to their specific spiritual gifts and their work, and not least of those who in the exercise of their functions for the building up of the Church were not limited to a particular locality. This fact accounts for the selection that we have here and in the similar list in 1 Corinthians xii. 28.

First stood the *apostles*. The word *apostolos* is used in three different ways in the New Testament. It could mean simply a messenger, as is the case apparently in Philippians ii. 25—we can neglect that meaning here. It was used above all for the twelve, who right on through the New Testament held a special and distinctive position (cf. 1 Cor. xv. 5; Rev. xxi. 14). But we read of others as apostles, not only Paul himself and Barnabas (Acts xiv. 14), but James the Lord's brother (Gal. i. 19), Silas (1 Thes. ii. 6), and Junias and Andronicus who are mentioned only in Romans xvi. 7. In fact there would appear to be those who can truly be called apostles (1 Cor. xv. 7), who are not even known to us by name. From Paul's words in 1 Corinthians ix. 1f. it would seem that a necessary quali- fication of an apostle was to have seen the risen Lord, and to have been sent out by Him, and thus to have come to be engaged as a foundation member (Eph. ii. 20) and worker for the building up of the Church.[1] If the qualification for an apostle was thus to have seen and been sent by the risen Lord, the proof of an apostle was his labours in the power of Christ, even 'by signs and wonders and mighty works' (2 Cor. xii. 12).

Closely associated with them in the work of building the Church from its foundations, and therefore basic as gifts of Christ to the Church, were the *prophets* (see on ii. 20 and iii. 5). It is harder for us to see their particular ministry, but they stand out clearly from the New Testament as men of inspired utterance, whose ministry of the word was of the utmost importance for the young Church. On occasion they might foretell the future, as in Acts xi. 28 and xxi. 9, 11, but like the Old Testament prophets their great work was to 'forth-tell' the word of God. This might be in bringing to light with convicting power the sins of men (1 Cor. xiv. 24ff.), or in bringing new strength to the Church by the word of exhorta- tion. The latter is illustrated most strikingly by Acts xv. 32 where it is said that in Antioch 'Judas and Silas, being prophets also themselves, exhorted the brethren with many words, and confirmed them.'

From the very definition of an apostle it is evident that their ministry must cease with the passing of the first generation from the Church. The ministry, or at least the name, of

---

[1] The phrase 'apostles of the churches' (2 Cor. viii. 23) may be taken in the non-technical sense as 'messengers'—the rendering given by AV, RV, RSV.

prophet also soon died in the Church. Their work, receiving and declaring the word of God under direct inspiration of the Spirit, was most vital before there was a Canon of New Testament Scripture. We read of prophets in the second century, but they have diminishing importance. The apostolic writings were coming to be read widely and accepted as authoritative, and this tended to replace the authority of the prophets. At the same time the local ministry was assuming much greater importance than that of itinerant ministers, and there was the added problem that there were many false teachers and self-styled 'prophets' who went from place to place to peddle their wares.

Next come the *evangelists*. Only two other references to these in the New Testament can guide us as to their function and work. In Acts xxi. 8 Philip, whose four daughters were prophets, is called an evangelist, and in 2 Timothy iv. 5 Timothy is told to 'do the work of an evangelist'. We may assume that theirs was an itinerant work of preaching under the apostles, and it may be fair to call them 'the rank and file missionaries of the Church' (Barclay).

Then, linked together (by the same article in the Greek) are the *pastors and teachers*. It is possible that this phrase describes the ministers of the local church, whereas the first three categories are regarded as belonging to the universal Church. More likely, the dominant thought is still of spiritual functions and gifts. Apostles and evangelists had a particular task in planting the Church in every place, prophets for bringing a particular word from God to a situation. Pastors and teachers were gifted to be responsible for the day-to-day building up of the Church. There is no hard and fast line to be drawn between the two. The duties of the pastor (literally 'shepherd') are to feed the flock with spiritual food and to see that they are protected from spiritual danger. Our Lord used the word in John x. 11, 14 to describe His own work, and He is ever the Chief Pastor (Heb. xiii. 20; 1 Pet. ii. 25, v. 4), under whom men are called to 'tend the flock of God' (1 Pet. v. 2; cf. Jn. xxi. 15ff., Acts xx. 28). Every pastor must be 'apt to teach' (cf. 1 Tim. iii. 2; cf. Tit. i. 9), though it is evident that some have pre-eminently the gift of teaching, and may be said to form a particular division of ministry within the Church, and to be a special gift of Christ to His people (Acts xiii. 1; Rom. xii. 7; 1 Cor. xii. 28).

12. Three phrases are now used in this verse to describe the purpose of the spiritual gifts just named. As different translations indicate, the three have been connected in various ways. The AV takes each of them separately. But the difference of the prepositions in the Greek is against this, and at least implies that the later two are dependent on the first. NEB is probably correct in making the second depend closely on the first, and the third on the two that precede: 'to equip God's people for work in his service, to the building up of the body of Christ'.

In the first place then, the ministry of the Church is given to it *for the perfecting of the saints*. The word used *(katartismos)* is not found elsewhere in the New Testament, although the corresponding verb is used of repairing something (Mt. iv. 21); of God's bringing the universe in the beginning into its intended shape and order (Heb. xi. 3); and of restoring to spiritual health a person who has fallen (Gal. vi. 1). It may be used, however, of 'perfecting' what is lacking in the faith of Christians (cf. 1 Thes. iii. 10; Heb. xiii. 21; 1 Pet. v. 10) and we may say with Robinson that the word denotes 'the bringing of the saints to a condition of fitness for the discharge of their functions in the Body, without implying restoration from a disordered state'. Their being brought to this condition is not an end in itself, but for a purpose, that they may be fitted *for the work of the ministry*. As clearly as in verse 7 it is thus implied that every Christian has a work of ministry, a spiritual task and function in the body. The word used here *(diakonia*; or the corresponding verb) is used of menial service (Lk. x. 40, xvii. 8, xxii. 26f.; Acts vi. 2), and so of the particular work of those who came to be known as 'deacons', but it is also used in the more general sense of our word 'service' (see iii. 7).

What is done for the saints, and by the saints, is *for the edifying of the body of Christ*. The word *oikodomē* has been used in

ii. 21, but here it has a broader meaning. The Church is increased and built up, and its members edified, as each member uses his particular gifts as the Lord of the Church ordains, and thus gives spiritual service to his fellow-members and to the Head. Because of its applied meaning the use of *oikodomē* with the *body* does not necessarily involve confusion of metaphors, but because of what he wishes to say now about the growth and unity of the Church, the apostle finds the metaphor of the body more adequate than any other.

13. All the three phrases in verse 12 have described the process going on in the life of the Church. But the apostle could never think of a process without fixing his eyes on the goal. The verb used at the beginning of the verse (*katantaō*) is used nine times in Acts for travellers arriving at their destination; NEB translates 'so shall we all at last attain . . .'. (Cf. Acts xxvi. 7 and Phil. iii. 11 for use similar to that here.) And the end of the Church's journey is described in three ways. First, it is *the unity of the faith*. Where *the faith* (see on verse 5) is duly communicated, people from their different backgrounds of error and ignorance come into a growing understanding of the 'one hope', an increasing dependence on the 'one Lord', and so to a developing appreciation of the 'one body'. The goal must be unity in the faith.

Secondly, it is emphasized, though enough has already been said to make this evident, that faith is not just the acceptance of a collection of dogmas, in the embracing of which unity will be found. It is something deeper and more personal. It is unity in *the knowledge of the Son of God* (see on i. 17). We can never know any person simply with our mind; and knowledge of such a Person as is envisaged here must involve the deepest possible fellowship. For this Person is *the Son of God*, and here we have one of the rare places in all the Pauline Epistles where this title is used (cf. Rom. i. 4; Gal. ii. 20; 1 Thes. i. 10). When Paul speaks of the relation of the Lord to His Church and to the Father's purpose, he regularly uses the title 'Christ', but 'when he would describe Him as the object of that faith and knowledge in which our unity will ultimately be realised'

(Robinson), he speaks of Him in His unique position as the Son of God.

But such knowledge which is fellowship with the Son of God involves the full experience of life 'in Christ', and therefore development *unto a perfect man, unto the measure of the stature of the fulness of Christ.* All the different expressions here speak of maturity. The word translated *perfect* (*teleios*) has the connotation of full development in 1 Corinthians ii. 6, xiv. 20 and Hebrews v. 14. *Man*hood here means adulthood, as in 1 Corinthians xiii. 11 where it is also contrasted with *nēpios*, the word used in the next verse here for children. The singular, moreover, expresses again the thought that maturity involves unity; the 'many' are to become 'one new man' (ii. 15). Then the word that is used for *stature*, which may connote age (Jn. ix. 21, 23) or physical stature (Lk. xix. 3), speaks figuratively of maturity, the measure of which is nothing less than *the fulness of Christ.* As in i. 23 some interpret it here as 'the measure of the perfect Christ', made complete by His fulfilment in His Church. Others take it as that which is filled by Christ. It seems better to understand it in the way that we have taken the phrase in i. 23, as the complete possession of the gifts and grace of Christ that He seeks to impart to man. He has Himself the very fullness of God (Col. i. 19, ii. 9); He seeks that the Christian should be filled with all of His endowment that can be communicated. Whether the goal can be realized in this life or not is irrelevant. The point is that the Christian is to press forward with no lesser ambition than this.

14. There must be *no more* the immaturity of children (*nēpioi*), characterized by instability in face of the pressures of different doctrines and standards of life. The word translated *tossed to and fro* is the verb from the noun *kludōn*, used in Luke viii. 24 of the raging of the waters of Galilee, and in James i. 6 for the 'surge of the sea' (RV); in the latter case it is the waves themselves that are driven by the wind, but here the picture is probably that of a boat tossed in the storm and *carried about.* This second verb is translated more vividly by NEB 'whirled about'; the Greek verb *peripherō* often has the idea of such violent swinging about as makes a person dizzy. The companion Epistle to the Colossians shows well that there were various *winds of doctrine* against which Christians were realizing already that they had to keep an even keel. The unsteady and rudderless could easily be turned from their course. For there were not only those who had been deceived and gone astray without realizing it, but there were some who were lying *in wait to deceive* (cf. 2 Tim. iii. 13). Their activities are described first by the word *kubia*, which means literally playing with dice, and hence trickery or fraud; and secondly as *cunning craftiness* (*panourgia*), the word used with reference to our Lord's questioners in Luke xx. 23, and in 2 Corinthians xi. 3 of the guile of the serpent. The AV translation of the last phrase of the verse is not as accurate as the RV, 'after the wiles of error'. When men wander out of the way of the truth (the Greek *planē*, 'error', is literally 'wandering'), they do not hesitate to use 'deceitful schemes' (NEB) and cunning devices to lead others to follow them.

15. The preachers of the truth for their part cannot and must not resort to such methods (2 Cor. iv. 2); they must act in all simplicity and straightforwardness, but at the same time beware of the means that their enemies may use. They are ambassadors of the truth, and are to be found *speaking the truth* and 'dealing truly' (RV mg.—the Greek word *alētheuō* includes both). Moreover, both are to be done *in love*. What is upheld, and the manner in which it is supported, are to be in complete contrast to the men spoken of in verse 14. Such deceive men to make their own gain; the Christian is to hold forth the truth in order to bring spiritual benefit to others, and he is to do so with a winsomeness that only love can make possible. Then with a metaphor which is as far as possible removed from that which describes the immature as tossed about like a little boat in a storm, it is said that they will *grow* in stability and spiritual maturity. That growth is *into* Christ, the development of the life so that it is found more and more 'in' Him, *all things* and every part of life finding their centre and object and goal in relation to Him and in union with Him. The preposition might

also be translated 'towards' or 'unto', and thus have the
thought of growth towards His perfect humanity as standard,
in the way that verse 13 has expressed it.

We should not imagine that the apostle thought of growth
into the Head. We are wise to take the imagery of growth first,
and then the thought of *Christ* as *the head*. He may be spoken
of as the whole Body, but also in a particular way as the Head.
This has been expressed already in i. 22, and will be again in
v. 23. Growth, and indeed every activity of the members, is
under His direction. The members can be healthy and strong
only as each is obedient to His control. The next verse develops this point.

16. *From* Christ alone, as Head, the body derives its whole
capacity for growth and activity, and its direction as one co-
ordinated, directed entity. Colossians ii. 19 is closely parallel
to this verse, and should be studied with it, but there the word
translated *fitly joined together* is not used. Its only other use in
the New Testament is in ii. 21. It derives from a word (*harmos*)
used for a joint or fastening in the construction of a building,
or for the shoulder-joint of the body. The second participle
(*sunbibazomenon*) is used in a general way of bringing things or
people together, and of reconciling those who have quarrelled,
and of putting together facts in an argument or a course of
teaching. Both participles thus give the sense of a functional
unity, that is made possible among the members by the
direction of the Head. But after the participles the Greek is
difficult. The word translated *joint* (*haphē*) has many meanings.
Basically it means a 'touch', and so can mean 'contact', 'point
of contact', or 'grip', and these meanings have led commentators to a variety of interpretations. Both the context and
medical usage of the word for a 'joint' of the body justify the
AV rendering, and most English translations follow this. The
Greek then would literally be taken 'through every joint of the
supply', and *that which every joint supplieth* is hardly possible as a
translation. Rather it is through every joint with which the
body is equipped—'every constituent joint' (NEB)—that
growth and true functioning is possible. In other words the

body depends for its growth and its work on the Lord's direction, on His provision for the whole (compare verses 11, 12), and on His arrangement for the inter-relation of the members as well.

Then we are brought back to a word that has become familiar in this Epistle (cf. i. 19 and iii. 7), as the apostle turns from the consideration of the members and the connection between them, to the *effectual working* of the whole. Each part, in its *measure* and according to its need, must have this functioning that is made possible by the 'energizing' of God in the whole. Then yet again the purpose of growth is mentioned, and it is made clear that each member does not seek its own growth, but that of *the body* as a whole, not its own *edifying*, but the *edifying* of the whole. We may translate, as RV does, 'building up', but the context makes clear that it is not increase in size of the Church that is primarily in view, by members being added to it, but spiritual increase. And this increase is above all *in love*. The little phrase comes yet again (cf. i. 4, iii. 17, iv. 2, v. 2), as love determines that each member will seek the upbuilding of all. Then without doubt, if there is a fellowship living in love and showing the truth in love, the numerical increase will follow.

IV. PERSONAL STANDARDS (iv. 17–v. 21)

a. New life to replace the old (iv. 17–24)

17, 18. This chapter began with a call to Christians to walk worthily of their vocation, and continued with the demand for spiritual growth in the fellowship of the Body of Christ. Now in still more practical terms Paul describes the way in which such a call is to be followed. There must be the complete abandonment of the old way of living, and the working out of the new in personal life, and also in human relationships. Though the old life has been renounced by the Christian minority, they are living surrounded by those who still *walk* (see on ii. 2) in the darkness of their godlessness. So a warning is necessary, and it is expressed in the strongest terms.

Therefore—that is, in the light of your high calling—*I say, and testify in the Lord.* This word *testify* (*marturomai*) is used (as in Acts xx. 26 and Gal. v. 3) to introduce a solemn declaration. NEB translates it, 'I urge it upon you'. Moreover it is from one who lives *in the Lord* to others whose life is so to be lived. He is writing to those who by race are Gentiles, but who, by the transforming grace of Christ, have come to be different from *other Gentiles*. In fact the reading which has the greatest support of the old MSS here omits the word *other*, to indicate that from being Gentiles before, they now in effect had become members of the Israel of God (Gal. vi. 16). In spiritual rather than racial terminology the implication here is that in the past they 'were Gentiles' (1 Cor. xii. 2), 'aliens from the commonwealth of Israel', with all that that involved (see ii. 12), but that they are so no longer.

The true nature of that old way of life is described now in a series of devastating phrases. It is true that there were some noble figures in the ancient world of Greece and Rome in which Paul lived, but the classical literature as it throws light on the life of the masses indicates that the apostle's description was not wide of the mark. (See Moule, *ES*, pp. 213ff.) There was a mental, spiritual and moral decadence in that society. Their way of life was vain (cf. 1 Pet. i. 18) because, as the apostle says, *vanity* was characteristic of *their mind*. 'In losing the living conception of a living God', pagan society had 'lost also the conception of the true object and perfection of human life; and so wandered on aimless, hopeless, reckless' (Barry). It is not implied that all that is said in this section is true of all who are not Christian, but it is not unfair to say that 'this is the direction in which every life is facing which is out of touch with God; and this is the kind of life which will be reproduced in a community in which Christian influence is not active.'[1] Without the knowledge of God, ultimately all is vanity, as there is no sense of purpose. There may be much knowledge (cf. Mt. xi. 25; 1 Cor. i. 18ff.), but there is no light of wisdom in the mind, the *understanding* is *darkened*. Then, as the knowledge of God involves more than the mind (see on verse 13),

[1] W. M. F. Scott, *op. cit.*, p. 63.

and since such knowledge means fellowship with Him, man's true life, ignorance of Him of necessity means *being alienated from the life of God* (cf. ii. 1). The word *alienated* may or may not convey the sense of being estranged from what was once possessed. From one standpoint it was no fault of their own if the saving and life-giving knowledge of God in Christ had not come to them. From another standpoint, they, in common with all men, had sinned against the light that they had (Rom. i. 18ff., ii. 12ff.). There had been a 'hardening of their heart' (RV) for which they could not disclaim all responsibility. The word rendered *blindness* by AV and 'hardening' by RV is one that is difficult to translate, and perhaps the meaning lies between the two renderings. The Greek noun *pōrōsis* could derive from an adjective meaning 'blind', but more likely is from a verb that means to 'petrify' or 'cause a callus to form', and so figuratively 'to become hard' or 'insensitive'. The noun that we have here, or the corresponding verb, is used eight times in the New Testament. The meaning 'blindness' does not always fit these contexts. In Mark iii. 5 and viii. 17 it refers to an attitude that is certainly culpable. 'Hardness' in the sense of 'stubbornness' may be a little too strong. As Robinson puts it, 'It seems not to indicate a stubborn refusal . . . and yet not an ignorance that is completely unblameworthy.'[1] The NEB translating 'their minds have grown hard as stone' gives the idea of an insensitivity to the finer things which characterizes a life that is lived without regard for God or for moral values.

19. The next expression carries on the thought of the callousness of the Gentiles. They showed themselves to be *past feeling*, to have ceased to have any appreciation of the truth of God or any feeling of shame in the face of evil. The original force of the word is to have no more pain or sorrow, and so can be applied here to indicate that 'they have deadened their conscience and do not feel its stings' (Lock) (cf. 1 Tim. iv. 2). Immorality of life has inevitably followed. They *have given themselves over*, 'abandoned themselves' (NEB), to a life that is a

---

[1] See Robinson, pp. 264ff., for a long discussion of the meaning and New Testament use of the word.

betrayal of their true selves. It is a life of *aselgeia*, a word that means 'licentiousness' or 'wanton violence' (*LS*), outrageous conduct of any kind, a life without any care for personal standards or social sanctions. Shamelessly they have given themselves *to work all* kinds of *uncleanness*. The noun for work, (*ergasia*) can mean (as in Acts xvi. 16, 19, xix. 24) business or the gains of business, and so the thought here may be that of making a trade of impurity (as RV mg. suggests). This, however, would be unfair as a description of the Gentile world in general, but at least the word implies that such uncleanness has become, as Moule puts it, an 'earnest pursuit' or 'occupation' (*CB*).

The word that follows (*pleonexia*), qualifying uncleanness, means essentially *greediness*, the desire for more than is one's due, and the passion to possess it without regard for what is right or for the persons of others. It does not always have the force that the word 'covetousness' (RV mg.) has acquired in English. In the use of the word in the New Testament it is often closely linked with the sins of the flesh. This is the case in all three passages where it is used in this Epistle (here and in v. 3, 5), and also in Colossians iii. 5 and 1 Thessalonians iv. 6 (the corresponding verb). It may be best to say that the word fundamentally means 'greed' for what is not one's due; sometimes in the New Testament it is used for the desire for money (Lk. xii. 15; 2 Cor. ix. 5), at other times its context gives it the force that it evidently has here of the passion for sexual indulgence at others' expense. In this connection see Hebrews xiii. 4, 5 where the thought of one kind of greed seems to lead naturally to the thought of the other.

20, 21. 'But you', the apostle says to his readers, emphasizing the personal pronoun, 'can no longer walk in that way. You *have not so learned Christ*. The truth of God and of His purpose has come to dominate your minds, and this truth has ethical implications. Your lives are no longer dark, your minds no longer vain. You are no longer alienated but walking step by step in the full light of the Lord, and in fellowship with Him. So you must finish with all immorality, and the passion for what is impure, and for what outrages the souls and bodies of others.'

Moreover those who have come to recognize that they are Christ's, have *heard him*, and *been taught by him*. Rather the original in this last clause is 'in him' repeating thus the key phrase of the Epistle. Christ was not only the subject, but 'the sphere of the instruction' (Robinson). With gentle irony the apostle adds force to his argument here. The *if so be that* is the same little word *eige* which we have had in iii. 2, not suggesting (as we have seen there) that they might not have heard, but rather calling 'the reader to verify the statement' (Moule, *CB*), and as a result to make sure that he in no way acts as if he had not heard the voice of the living Christ in his heart. They had accepted the fact that *the truth is in Jesus*, the truth about God, about the world, and the true way that they ought to live. 'When you learnt Christ', the apostle would say, 'you learnt the truth; and it was in the incarnate Jesus, in His words and in His life' (cf. Jn. xiv. 6). This seems the best way to take these words, thus dependent on the whole of verses 20, 21. It is possible, however, and without essential difference of meaning, to take them with what follows. The Greek would permit such a translation as 'The truth in Jesus'—that is, the true way for man that is revealed in Him—'is that you *put off* . . .'.

22. The metaphor that we have here to express the change of life that there is when a person comes to be 'in Christ' is a familiar Pauline and early Christian one. Indeed it is so frequent in the New Testament Epistles (e.g. Rom. xiii. 12; Col. iii. 9; Heb. xii. 1; Jas. i. 21; 1 Pet. ii. 1) that it is one of those things that have led to the suggestion of the existence even in apostolic times of a basic Christian catechism containing material that was used in the instruction of catechumens as to the meaning of new life in Christ.[1] The old is to be *put off* and the new to be *put on;* and if a figure taken from dress might seem to indicate a merely superficial change, we should see the point as the complete setting aside of the old 'garments',

[1] See p. 27 and E. G. Selwyn, *op. cit.*, pp. 393ff.

having nothing further to do with them, and replacing them by new ones. What is to be *put off* is described as *the old man*. As past sins are dealt with by the grace of forgiveness, and as repentance determines to abandon them completely, all that belongs to the old way of life, the way of the heathen that has been described in verses 17–19, is to be set aside decisively. (The Greek aorist signifies a single act.) That 'manner of life' (RSV) was *corrupt* and corrupting. The participle may mean 'perishing' (cf. Rom. viii. 21; 2 Cor. iv. 16; Gal. vi. 8) or 'rotten' and 'polluted' (cf. 2 Cor. xi. 3). Perhaps both meanings are present here (see note on the negative of the same root in vi. 24.) The *lusts*, the self-centred desires that belong to that old way of life, are *deceitful* in that they promise joy and gain but cannot fulfil the promise. The whole Bible, from the story of man's first temptation, presents the persuasion to sin as deceit (cf. Mt. xiii. 22; Rom. vii. 11; Heb. iii. 13). It leads to the pollution and the spoiling of what God has made and planned, and in the end causes the doer to perish in it (Jn. iii. 16; 2 Thes. ii. 10).

23. The 'old man' is to be put off, and the Christians are to be *renewed*. Greek has two adjectives for new: *kainos*, which means new in the sense of fresh, and *neos*, which means new in the sense of young. Both have corresponding verbs that are used in the New Testament concerning life in Christ. In 2 Corinthians iv. 16 and Colossians iii. 10 there is that which is formed from *kainos*, which thus has the sense of the new creation of God, replacing that which is old by a new kind of life that was not known before (see on ii. 15). Here we have the verb from *neos*, which thus implies 'putting off the decrepitude of the old man' and the 'regaining' of 'undying youth' (Barry). The present tense emphasizes further that what is required, and made possible in Christ, is continuous renewal. The place of this constant renewal or rejuvenation is *the spirit of the mind*. The construction here impels us to take *pneuma* as the human spirit and not the divine Spirit, though the expression is without parallel in the New Testament. The mind is the centre of a person's thinking, but as the apostle regards it, it can be used to think spiritual things or merely natural things. It can dwell on vanity (verse 17, and cf. Col. ii. 18), but it can also be lifted to spiritual things. Such renewal in the mind (Rom. xii. 2) or in *the spirit of* the *mind*, is possible by the indwelling of the Spirit of God. Then indeed there will be a new way of thinking, and in consequence a new way of life.

24. Now *kainos*, the second word for new, is used; for in the place of the old nature, characterized by selfishness and sin, and bound by evil and its consequences, there is the *new man*, the new nature, which is God's creation (see on ii. 10, 15, and cf. 2 Cor. v. 17; Gal. vi. 15; Col. iii. 10; Tit. iii. 5). Here, moreover, the aorist verb implies the decisive act of putting on this God-created, God-given life, as it has already implied the decisive putting off of the old. The two truths of this verse and the last need to be kept before the Christian man. As Westcott puts it, 'Two things are required for the positive formation of the Christian character, the continuous and progressive renewal of our highest faculty, and the decisive acceptance of "the new man".' This *new man* is created *after God*. That could be taken as meaning 'according to God's will and purpose', but the parallel in Colossians iii. 10, by its greater fullness, must be taken to interpret this. There 'the new man' is said to be 'renewed in knowledge after the image of him that created him'. Man was made in His image in the beginning (Gn. i. 27), and when that image had been marred by sin and the life in fellowship with God lost, there was in Christ a new creation, a restoration to the divine image with all that that means. Above all, the image of God is shown in character *in righteousness and . . . holiness*. If these qualities are not seen, at least in some measure, there is no evidence that there has been God's work of re-creation at all. In Philo and Plato, as well as in the New Testament, 'righteousness' is used of the fulfilment of duty to man, and 'holiness' of observing one's duty to God. (In Lk. i. 75; 1 Thes. ii. 10, and Tit. i. 8, as here, the two words, or their cognate forms, stand together.) The AV takes the genitive 'of truth' (RV) or more strictly 'of the truth' simply as an adjective, *true*. The presence of the article in particular is against the AV translation. Probably there is a deliberate contrast between what has been said already (especially in verse 22) to be the fruit of deceit, and such righteousness and holiness as come into the character when the truth as it is in Jesus is embraced and followed. (Compare the similar contrast in verses 14, 15.) NEB speaks of 'the new nature of God's creating, which shows itself in the just and devout life called for by the truth'.

b. Truth and love to replace falsehood and bitterness (**iv. 25–v. 2**)

25. The last section has spoken in general terms of the putting off of the old life characterized by ignorance, vanity and deceit, and so impurity and lust. In its place there must be put on the new man, that means a new way of life characterized by holiness and righteousness. In this section the apostle turns to speak quite specifically of the sins that are to be put off, and the positive qualities or types of action that must be found in the Christian's life. First, in contrast to the word 'truth' that ends verse 24, he turns to speak of the way that 'falsehood' (RV) must be put away. AV has *lying*, and it is probably the speaking of what is untrue that is particularly, though not solely, in mind (see on the opposite quality in verse 15). For in place of such falsehood, the duty to *speak every man truth with his neighbour* is to be recognized. These words are a quotation of the LXX of Zechariah viii. 16, but with a significant little change. The preposition 'to' becomes *with*, thus 'bringing out more closely the union of man with man' (Lock) that is emphasized in the clause that follows.

We are members one of another. For his argument against falsehood, Paul does not simply appeal to the moral law that his readers knew well.[1] Rather he insists that Christians break the bonds of love and fellowship by which they have come to be bound, when they try to deceive one another. They belong

[1] For a valuable study of the basis of Pauline ethics, and of the arguments that Paul gives, especially in this Epistle, for ethical conduct, see Findlay, pp. 305ff.

together as members of the one body (cf. Rom. xii. 5), and so must be completely honest one with another. Chrysostom aptly says, 'If the eye sees a serpent, does it deceive the foot? if the tongue tastes what is bitter, does it deceive the stomach?' Lying is a gross hindrance to the proper functioning of the body. When members are open and perfectly truthful one with another, the body will work in harmony and therefore efficiently. Without openness and truth, there can only be disunity, disorder and trouble.

26. Another mark of the old nature is plain bad temper, unjustified anger. Quoting the Old Testament again, the LXX of Psalm iv. 4, he says, *Be ye angry, and sin not.* The English rendering 'Stand in awe, and sin not' gives a different turn to it. The Hebrew verb *ragaz* means basically to 'tremble', and it could be with fear or rage *(BDB)*. Whichever was the psalmist's thought, the LXX is meaningful and relevant. There is anger which is righteous anger, such as we see in our Lord Himself (e.g. Mk. iii. 5; Jn. ii. 13–17); but His anger never led to sin, because His emotions were kept under perfect control. The Christian must be sure that his anger is that of righteous indignation, and not just an expression of personal provocation or wounded pride. It must have no sinful motives, nor be allowed to lead to sin in any way.

Moreover, the apostle, with his sure knowledge of human nature, is aware that what begins as righteous anger 'against sins' very easily becomes perverted and soured and 'is turned against our brethren' (Calvin). Therefore he adds the wise practical instruction, *let not the sun go down upon your wrath.* There is a noteworthy change in the word used here. It is more strictly 'provocation', (*parorgismos*; the corresponding verb is used in vi. 4), the personal resentment that righteous anger can become when harboured and brooded over in men's hearts that are so stormed by temptations to malice and bitterness. Passionate feelings against people or their actions are not to be kept long, lest they break down the love that seeks to bring good out of evil. It is possible that Paul in giving this advice was consciously following what the Pythagoreans recommended. Plutarch said that 'if betrayed into angry reviling (they) made it their rule to shake hands before sunset'. But perhaps Psalm iv. 4 was still in his mind. For that verse quoted goes on, 'Commune with your own heart upon your bed, and be still', and Paul knew that such communing was impossible unless a man had set aside his anger before turning to his bed.

27. This verse is perhaps to be linked closely with what has gone before. The danger of anger is that it gives a *place* or opportunity *to the devil*. It gives him 'a half-open door' (Moule, *CB*), an opportunity of fostering the spirit of pride or hatred. Sudden instinctive indignation against injustice or wrong, good in itself, if retained and nursed as a grievance (NEB), will let the devil lead his victim on to unkind thoughts, words and actions, and so work havoc with personal relationships. The devil is to be resisted (Jas. iv. 7), and given no place whether it is the individual's spiritual life, or the welfare of the fellowship that is in danger (cf. 1 Pet. v. 8f.). As we have noted,[1] Paul usually employs the word 'Satan' for the evil one, and not *the devil*. This has led some, at least from the time of Erasmus and Luther, to take the word *diabolos* in the literal sense of 'slanderer', but the use of the word in vi. 11 and the common non-Pauline use suggests the alternative.

28. Turning to another characteristic of the old life, at least in some of his readers, he says *let him that stole steal no more*. There were those in the communities to which he addressed himself, as Paul makes specific in 1 Corinthians vi. 10f., who had been in the habit of making a living by pilfering (the present participle in the Greek implies this rather than a thief in any other sense). There must be no more of such practices, but honest toil instead. The word for this (*kopiaō*) signifies the strenuous work that produces fatigue, a word used in 1 Timothy iv. 10 and v. 17 for earnest Christian service, but used for Paul's own manual labour in 1 Corinthians iv. 12. The Christian is never to be ashamed or afraid of hard work; it is the duty of all (1 Thes. iv. 11; 2 Thes. iii. 10–12).

[1] See p. 35.

Moreover, rejecting all that in any past employment has been dishonest in any shape or form, he is to be *working with his hands the thing which is good*. Thus yet again Paul turns from the negative to the positive. Instead of robbing others of the fruit of their labour, the Christian is to work for his own living. More than that, he is to work to earn *that he may have to give to him that needeth*. The Christian motive for earning is not merely to have enough for oneself and one's own, and then perhaps for comforts and luxuries, but to have to give to those in need. The Christian philosophy of labour is thus lifted far above the thought of what is right or fair in the economic field; it is lifted to the place where there is no room for selfishness or the motive of personal profit at all. Giving becomes the motive for getting. We may note the place that giving to the poor had with our Lord and His disciples, in precept and practice, though their resources must have been very slender (Mt. xix. 21; Lk. xiv. 13; Jn. xiii. 29). Then from the beginning the Church felt a great responsibility in this direction (Acts ii. 44f., iv. 32ff., vi. 1ff.). Paul himself laid great emphasis on provision for the poor (Rom. xv. 26f.; 2 Cor. viii and ix; Gal. ii. 10), and was an example, in spite of all his labours in the ministry of the word, both in working with his hands for his own support (1 Thes. ii. 9; 2 Thes. iii. 8f.), and also in supporting others in need (Acts xx. 34f.).

29. Now the apostle turns back to consider the Christian's speech and conversation. Not only is he to shun 'lying' and all that is deceitful, but all 'bad language' (NEB). The adjective used in the Greek (*sapros*) basically means 'rotten', and then has a derived sense of 'worthless'. It is talk that is 'rotten' and that 'spreads rottenness' (Barry) like bad fruit; worthless and leading others to think on the worthless. To replace this there is to be what can be described plainly and simply as *that which is good* (cf. Phil. iv. 8). The AV *to the use of edifying* here does not quite translate the Greek. The word *chreia* means, as in Acts vi. 3, a 'matter in hand', and so here we might translate literally 'for the edifying of the matter in hand'—'words suitable for the occasion', Phillips aptly turns it. The thought is that of Proverbs xv. 23, 'A word spoken in due season, how good is it!' (Cf. Ecclus. xx. 6f., 19.) As with the consideration of work and wages, the Christian standard is lifted above personal expediency, even above the question of moral right or wrong. The test of a man's use of money is, 'What am I giving to those in need?' The test of his conversation is not just 'Am I keeping my words true and pure?' but 'Are my words being used to *minister grace unto the hearers*?' The *grace* of the Lord's own words, the love and blessing which they conveyed, is spoken of in Luke iv. 22. The utterance of the Christian is to be characterized by the same grace (cf. Col. iii. 16, iv. 6).

30. The instructions about anger were followed by the warning against giving place to the devil. These instructions now about the Christian's conversation are followed by the warning *grieve not the holy Spirit of God*. All sin—the reminder is necessary—and not least that of the tongue, is a cause of personal sorrow to God, for we are called to fellowship with Him. The reference to the Spirit, rather than to Christ or to the Father—probably derived from Isaiah lxiii. 10—is particularly apt in that the Spirit is the bond of the life of fellowship, and the sin of offending a brother by false word or act especially grieves Him. Perhaps also, as Robinson suggests, the Spirit 'specially claims to find expression in the utterances of Christians' (see v. 18f.), and 'the misuse of the organ of speech is accordingly a wrong done to, and felt by, the Spirit who claims to control it.' Then the AV indicates another point which the Greek forces on us. We are so accustomed to the 'Holy Spirit' as a title for the third Person of the Trinity that we forget the significance of the adjective, thrown into emphasis in the Greek here, and so kept as an adjective *holy* rather than as a title in the AV. The Spirit of God who indwells us now is holy. Furthermore by Him Christians *are sealed unto the day of redemption*. The Spirit's presence now is the seal and assurance of the life and inheritance that the Christian will possess fully in the end, and the very contemplation of that should lead him to purify his life (1 Jn. iii. 2f.). There may be here the thought also of the work of the Spirit as keeping the Christian inviolate under His seal for the day of redemption (Scott).

31. Once more the apostle turns back to those sins that so readily find expression in speech, in order finally to set over against them the way that has been learnt in Christ. Six things are named here decisively to be *put away*. First there is *bitterness* (*pikria*), which Aristotle spoke of as 'the resentful spirit which refuses reconciliation'. In his typical way the apostle says that *all* of this (see on iv. 2) must go, every trace of such sharpness of temper. Then come *wrath* (*thumos*) and *anger* (*orgē*), named together also in Romans ii. 8 and Colossians iii. 8 (cf. Rev. xvi. 19, xix. 15), and to be distinguished as the outburst of passion (cf. Lk. iv. 28; Acts xix. 28) is from the settled feeling of anger. *Orgē* is used for the wrath of God (see v. 6), and the verb is used in verse 26 for the righteous anger of man. Here it is used for the anger that springs from personal animosity, the flaring up of passion and temper because of personal provocation; and the only Christian rule concerning this is total abstinence. Then follows the word *kraugē*, translated *clamour*, 'the loud self-assertion of the angry man, who will make every one hear his grievance' (Findlay). *Evil speaking* translates the Greek *blasphēmia*, a word often used in the Bible for speaking against God, but also common for slanderous or abusive speaking against one's fellow men (cf. 1 Cor. x. 30; Col. iii. 8; Tit. iii. 2). Lastly the apostle adds *all malice*, 'bad feeling of every kind' (NEB), thus demanding the complete exclusion from the Christian's life of every thought that leads a person to speak or do evil against another.

32. The eradication of evil words and actions depends ultimately on the purification of the thought life. So, speaking positively, the apostle says, *be ye kind one to another, tender-hearted.* . . . The parallel Colossians iii. 12 says, 'Put on therefore, as God's elect, holy and beloved, a heart of compassion, kindness, humility, meekness, longsuffering' (RV). Three of these Paul has spoken of in this chapter in verse 2; here he dwells on the others. Kindness, used of God in ii. 7, is urged here as a fundamental Christian virtue. It is love in practical action; as Barclay puts it, it is 'the disposition of mind which thinks as much of its neighbour's affairs as it does of its own'. In adding *tenderhearted* (*eusplanchnoi*) a word used elsewhere in the New Testament only in 1 Peter iii. 8, the apostle makes sure that he cannot be understood as requiring acts of kindness without a heart of sympathy and love prompting them (cf. 1 Cor. xiii. 1f.).

He knows, however, that the obstacle to kindness and compassion is often the sense of wrong done to one, or a grievance nursed; so he goes on to speak of *forgiving one another*. The word can have the wider meaning of 'dealing graciously' one with another, but this includes forgiveness, which is probably the dominant thought here. In Colossians iii. 13 the addition 'if any man have a quarrel against any' makes this meaning quite specific. The supreme example and motive for all Christian forgiveness is God's own forgiveness. 'God . . . in Christ', the RV rightly translates (cf. 2 Cor. v. 19), 'forgave you.' He has done this once and for all and completely. Therefore men in love and gratitude to Him must forgive. The Gospels indeed emphasize that God's forgiveness cannot be received by the heart which is itself unforgiving (see e.g. Mt. vi. 12, 14f., xviii. 21–35). But the *even as* (*kathōs*) means more than 'because'; there is to be a real likeness between the forgiveness of God and the Christian's forgiving. The latter is to be as free and complete as His who puts away a man's sins as far as the east is from the west, and holds them against him no more.[1]

v.1. In this matter of forgiving, the calling of Christians is to be *followers of God*. In fact *mimētai* is more than *followers*. It is 'imitators' (RV), a word used a number of times in the New

---

[1] Here and in the next verse the MSS vary between 'us' and 'you', and it is not possible to be sure which was written originally in each place. 'One reason why Greek manuscripts oscillate so much between *hēmeis* ("we") and *hymeis* ("you") is that the pronunciation of these two pronouns was almost identical in the first century A.D. and onwards. Hence if a scribe was copying by dictation, he might well put the one for the other, especially in a context like this, where either pronoun makes good sense' (Bruce).

Testament for the following of a human example, but only here of imitating God Himself. Furthermore, the verb is more strictly 'become'. Those who by grace are made *children* of God are by constant perseverance, and imitation of the divine copy (cf. 1 Pet. ii. 21), to become more like the heavenly Father (cf. Mt. v. 44f., 48; Lk. vi. 36). Given the unbelievable privilege and grace of being His 'beloved', they are to respond in showing 'self-forgetting kindness' (Moule, *CB*).

2. In fact the apostle would broaden the sphere of 'imitation of God' from simply the forgiving spirit to *love* in every other way. The constancy with which such love is to be demonstrated is indicated by yet another use of the word *walk* (see on ii. 2). Love is to characterize the Christian's daily progress along the road of life. Indeed this verse sums up the whole section, and sets aside all the negatives with its one great positive command. There is a perfect example, even in human flesh, which has been given and can be copied. Love answering love, love motivated by love, love made possible by the initial love of Christ, is one of the great themes of the Johannine literature (see Jn. xiii. 34; 1 Jn. iv. 10f., etc.); but Paul has it too.

As in iv. 32, the conjunction *kathōs* indicates a standard of comparison, and particular practical outworkings of love seen in the life of Christ are to be followed in the life of the Christian. His love was expressed in giving, and that to the point of sacrifice (cf. Gal. ii. 20). The implication is that the Christian's love is similarly to be expressed in giving and sacrifice. In verse 25 of this chapter the apostle applies this to the love of husbands for their wives. In 1 John iii. 16 it is made to apply generally, and that verse says more specifically what is implied here, namely that His laying down His life demands the response of our laying down 'our lives for the brethren' (cf. Jn. xv. 12f.). However, there is not a single place in Paul's writings, nor in the New Testament generally, where the death of Christ can be spoken of as only an example to be followed, without the further expression of its atoning significance. This is stated here when it is said that *for us* He died, presenting Himself *an offering and a sacrifice to God*. There is no point in the argument of some commentators that the reference to His offering Himself is here unrelated to man's need of forgiveness. It is not directly connected with the exhortation of iv. 32, but the terms of the Old Testament sacrificial ritual are used, and His death is described as being *for us*.

The two words here, *prosphora* and *thusia*, are used together in the LXX of Psalm xl. 6 (quoted in Heb. x. 5), and the former may perhaps be taken to refer to the whole life of obedience, and the latter in particular to His sacrificial death, but New Testament usage does not permit us to stress this distinction. The leading thought here is concerning that which in the beloved Son, and so in those who in Him are 'beloved children', pleases the Father. The Old Testament sacrifices were spoken of as a 'sweet savour', to express metaphorically their acceptability before God (Gn. viii. 21; Ex. xxix. 18, 25, 41; Lv. i. 9, 13, 17). To an infinitely higher degree was the sacrifice of Christ pleasing to the Father. To our eyes the cross can only present, as F. B. Meyer says, an 'awful scene of horror', but 'in love so measureless, so reckless of cost, for those who were naturally unworthy of it', there was an action that 'filled heaven with fragrance'.[1] So by implication the life that a man in Christ lives in sacrificial self-giving to God and to his fellows has a fragrance before God and in the world. The other two Pauline uses of the same expression illustrate the point. To the apostle such was the fragrance of the gifts of the Christians in Philippi (Phil. iv. 18), and thus he thought of his own life-calling, to be 'a sweet savour of Christ unto God' (2 Cor. ii. 14–16, RV), and to 'spread abroad the fragrance of the knowledge of (Christ)' (NEB); (cf. also Jn. xii. 3).

c. Light to replace darkness (v. 3–14)

3. In iv. 17–24 Paul has spoken in general terms of putting off the old man and putting on the new. In the last section (iv. 25–v. 2) he has spoken more particularly of putting aside

---

[1] F. B. Meyer, *Ephesians: A Devotional Commentary* (1953 reprint), p. 48.

deceitfulness and personal animosities, and of their replacement by truth and love in word, thought and action. Now suddenly we are turned from the contemplation of the self-giving, sacrificial love of Christ, to love's perversion in adultery and sexual abuse. The apostle knew the dangers to which his readers were exposed in the life of their society, and so spoke frankly about them.[1] 'Immorality' (RSV) and sexual perversion of almost every kind might be included under the word *porneia*, translated *fornication* in AV; it involves all that works against the life-long union of one man and one woman within the sanctity of the marriage bond. Such immorality may be regarded either as *uncleanness*, or as *covetousness* (NEB 'ruthless greed') in the sense in which the word *pleonexia* has been used already in iv. 19. The *or* supports our argument in the comment on that verse that 'greed' is being applied in these passages specially to the 'sins of the flesh'. Immorality is uncleanness or impurity because purity means the control and direction of sexual powers and impulses in accordance with the law and purpose of God. It is 'ruthless greed' because it is selfish indulgence at the expense of others. Such abuse of God-given powers and such contradiction of the loveliness of God's pattern of living should *not* even *be once named among* them. The expression recalls the Old Testament prohibition of mentioning even the names of the gods of the heathen, and of speaking of the manner of their worship (Ex. xxiii. 13; Dt. xii. 30; Ps. xvi. 4). It is incongruous for those who are called to be *saints* (see on i. 1) to take any pleasure in talking about such things, by their conversation to approve or condone, or by gossip to make light of the sins of others, or to excite sexual passion in the unwary (see also verse 12).

4. Before he turns to the positive side the apostle uses three more words to describe the conduct and conversation that is to have no place in the Christian's life. First there is *filthiness* (*aischrotēs*), more general than the *aischrologia*, 'filthy speech',

---

[1] Barclay (pp. 191f., 199ff.) gives a picture of the life of the Graeco-Roman and Jewish world that is very relevant as a background to Paul's instructions here, and to his words on marriage in verses 22-33.

of Colossians iii. 8. All that is shameless, all that would make a morally sensitive man ashamed (cf. Rom. vi. 21), must be excluded. Then he forbids *foolish talking*, the kind of talk, Plutarch says, that comes from a drunken man, words without either sense or profit. Also forbidden is *jesting*, distinguished by Findlay from the previous word as the idle talk of the clever man is from that of the stupid. The usage of this word *eutrapelia* in classical Greek was not derogatory. It could mean 'versatility' or 'witty repartee', but the context here indicates what is *not convenient* for the Christian man; probably Paul was thinking of 'the lightness of witty talk' that plays 'too often on the border-line of impropriety' (Robinson).

With a play on words he urges the replacing of *eutrapelia* by *eucharistia*—'let the grace of wit be superseded by the truer grace of thanksgiving', Robinson turns it. Calvin and others have taken *eucharistia* to mean 'gracious speech', and iv. 29 has spoken of the replacement of 'corrupt speech' by conversation that gives 'grace'. The Greek noun is not known to have been used with this wider meaning, though the corresponding adjective was so used. At least we may take it as *giving of thanks* in the widest sense. Paul will have more to say about the grace of gratitude in verse 20. Here he wants to insist that thanksgiving is the best use of speech. He does not prudishly forbid speaking about sex, nor austerely debar humour, but he would have none of the 'flippant talk' (NEB) that harms the spiritual life. Rather he would demand that if conversation is about sex, or possessions, or people, it should be directed by the spirit of thanksgiving and praise (cf. Heb. xiii. 15; 1 Pet. iv. 11), towards seeing and acknowledging the loveliness and beauty of God's gifts. If this is the case, then speech will be kept pure and uplifting.

5, 6. The apostle has solemn words to say about the consequences of such sins as those he has just enumerated in the lives of men. They, in common with all unrepented sins, exclude men from God's kingdom. *This ye know*, he says, using two verbs in a way that might best be rendered, 'Ye know, recognizing the truth of it' (Lock). Or the verb may be imperative, and the meaning 'be very sure of this' (NEB). They had been taught this from their first hearing of the Christian gospel, but they must *let no man deceive* them. There were then, as there always are, those who made light of sin, and scoffed at the thought of its consequences; but perhaps Paul was writing in the particular realization that among his readers were those representatives of early Gnosticism who said that the sins of the flesh were irrelevant to the spiritual life, and those too who took freedom from the law to mean liberty to continue in sin of any kind (cf. Rom. vi. 1). The words of such men, he would insist, were *vain words*. The word of God is solemn and true. *No whoremonger, nor unclean person, nor covetous man, who is an idolater, hath any inheritance in the kingdom of Christ and of God.* Only by the forsaking of sin in true repentance is the way open by faith for men to have inheritance in God's kingdom. Otherwise, *because of these things* men remain *children of disobedience* rather than children of God (see on ii. 2), 'children of wrath' (ii. 3) rather than inheritors of God's kingdom by grace. Apart from the gift of forgiveness, men stand under the wrath of God because of sin, subject to His judgment, which in part is a present fact in that they are even now excluded from the life of God (cf. Rom. i. 18–32), but in greater part waits for that day when all shall stand before their Lord and Judge.

In the naming of particular sins, we have essentially the same words as in verse 3, and the same connection of the word for *covetousness* or 'greed' with sexual immorality. There is, however, the further equation of this sin of 'greed' with idolatry (cf. Col. iii. 5). For passion, whether for money or for sexual indulgence, is in effect putting an idol and object of desire and worship before God. To the Jew idolatry was the worst of sins, and perhaps Bruce is right in saying that 'The part which the commandment against covetousness played in Paul's own spiritual experience (Rom. 7. 7ff.) no doubt made him acutely aware of the special deadliness of this subtle sin.' The solemn warning of judgment that is connected here with the 'sins of the flesh' raises certain questions in the minds of many. Are these sins worse than all others? Is it implied that sexual sin is the unforgivable sin, that debars man irrevocably from the kingdom of God? The very similar Pauline passages, 1 Corinthians vi. 9–11 and Colossians iii. 5ff., answer the second question. Paul could tell his readers that some of them had been guilty of these sins once, but now they were made new, pardoned, cleansed. Indeed we cannot say that these sins are viewed in the New Testament as worse than the sins of pride and the subtler forms of self-centredness. But neither Law nor Prophets in the Old Testament, nor Gospels nor Epistles in the New Testament, allow men to regard lightly the sins that break the bonds of marriage, destroy the sanctity of the family, and cause children to be brought to birth without parents to be responsible for their nurture and training. Finally a word should be said on the form of the expression *the kingdom of Christ and of God*. God's kingdom is Christ's kingdom. Christ is not explicitly called God, but in the construction here the two are included under the one definite article in such a way that, as Westcott puts it, they are brought 'into a connexion incompatible with a simply human view of the Lord's Person (comp. Tit. ii. 13; 2 Pet. i. 1)'.

7. *Therefore*, in the light of God's judgment and of the incompatibility of such sins with membership in the kingdom of God, Paul calls on his readers not to *be* (literally 'become') *partakers with them*. To join cause with such shameless sinners, with the 'sons of disobedience', is an utter denial of their Christian profession, and the warning is implied that it involves the danger of sharing the same consequences of sin in God's judgment.

8. At this point Paul brings in one of the most common and most striking New Testament illustrations of the absoluteness of the difference between the old heathen life and the life 'in Christ'. 'God is light' (1 Jn. i. 5). Light expresses His majesty and glory (1 Tim. vi. 16) and His perfect holiness, but also the truth that He wills to reveal Himself to man (Ps. xliii. 3). The opposite of that glory and holiness and wisdom of God is darkness, and the world estranged from God dwells in such darkness (see on i. 18). Those who have found life 'in Christ' are essentially people who have been transferred from the realm of darkness to the realm of light (Acts xxvi. 18; Rom. xiii. 12; 2 Cor. iv. 6; Col. i. 13; 1 Pet. ii. 9). Both in the Acts of the Apostles and in the Epistles we can see the great part that this symbolism played in the preaching and teaching of Paul in particular.

The special point to be noticed here is that he does not simply say, 'You were in darkness before'; there was indeed some light in the world around them, as God had not left Himself without a witness. He says rather that 'darkness was . . . in them' (Abbott). You *were . . . darkness*, he says. Their lives, and not just their environment, were dark. *But now*, he continues, you are *light in the Lord*. He says in effect, 'If you are in the Lord, you are in the light, and the light is in you.' They had received the light, and become luminous themselves (cf. Mt. v. 14). Again the apostle's command is, 'Be what you are. You have become light. You may be called *children of light*, those whose very nature is light.' They are to pursue their daily lives in accordance with this new nature given to them in Christ, and to express this most effectively the apostle once again uses the word *walk* (see on ii. 2). In the light that illuminates the pathway of God's will, and with light in their hearts, and radiating forth from their lives, they are to go on life's journey.

9. The same thing can be described in another way as bearing 'the fruit of the light'. This reading, accepted by all the recent Versions, has better MS authority than the AV *fruit of the Spirit*, though the earliest authority we have for Ephesians (the Chester Beatty papyrus) favours the AV reading and thus indicates that the change to *Spirit* must have been made very early. Paul may not be consciously thinking of the light as the seed planted in the life, and in due course having fruit there, but rather of the natural results that should follow, the kind of character that should be seen in the life of the person who has been illumined by Christ. In many passages *righteousness* is spoken of as a fruit of the life in Christ (e.g. Rom. vi. 21f.;

Phil. i. 11; Heb. xii. 11). All that is corrupt and unjust in man's relationships with his fellows (see on iv. 24) must have no place. Then instead of 'all malice' (iv. 31) there is to be *all goodness*, the active seeking of good in every part of life. There is an instructive distinction between 'goodness' and 'righteousness' in Romans v. 7, showing that the former adds to moral uprightness and integrity the attractiveness of a beautiful character. Thirdly, when the darkness of ignorance and blindness, error and deceit goes (iv. 14, 17f., 22), there is *truth* as the fruit of the light Christ brings.

10. Their life as children of light, moreover, was to involve a *proving* of *what is acceptable unto the Lord*. Verse 9 is parenthetical, and so this is connected closely with verse 8. In the matter of daily life and decisions they had to find out and act on the will of God. The thought is to be developed further in verse 17. The participle here (*dokimazontes*) is from a verb that sometimes means 'approving' (as in Rom. xiv. 22 and 1 Cor. xvi. 3), but more commonly 'proving' for oneself, and so here 'choosing'. It indicates the demand for careful thought and discrimination. The light of God is given, but it does not free men from the responsibility of thought and choice. Romans xii. 2 is most closely similar to this as it speaks of proving 'what is that good, and acceptable, and perfect, will of God'. In both places *acceptable* (*eurestos*) is better rendered by the more personal 'well-pleasing' (RV). The desires and choices of him who walks in the light are governed by his prior determination, to please not himself (Gal. i. 10), but his Lord (2 Cor. v. 9; Phil. iv. 18; Col. i. 10).

11–13. The old life that was 'darkness' was essentially *unfruitful* (cf. Rom. vi. 21). The apostle does not set one kind of fruit over against another. It is a matter of fruit or no fruit in the sight of God; wheat or tares; a harvest of good, or merely works—the endless, strenuous but futile striving of man instead of the natural development of the life of God within that leads to its outward manifestation in ways which are a blessing to all (Gal. v. 16 ff.). Since the darkness has been banished by the coming of the light, there must be *no fellowship* with the old. In verse 7 Paul has forbidden Christians to be sharers with the ungodly; here he emphasizes that they must 'take no part' (NEB) in their works.

The responsibility of the Christian with regard to the works of the ungodly is *rather to reprove them*. The verb *elenchō* is one that has a wide range of meanings, and so the context must help to guide us for its interpretation here. Originally it meant to 'disgrace' or 'put to shame'; then it had the sense of examining in order to reprove or convict, and so also to 'bring to the proof' or to 'confute' (*LS*). The New Testament speaks of people being convicted by the law (Jas. ii. 9), by conscience (Jn. viii. 9), and by the working of the Spirit (Jn. xvi. 8). This is not quite the meaning here. Nor can it be simply *reprove*, as it clearly is in Luke iii. 19, and in such passages as 1 Timothy v. 20 and Titus ii. 15, where it is shown that the Christian leader's duty is to rebuke specific sins. For the next verse here (in a way similar to verse 3) continues, *For it is a shame even to speak of those things which are done of them in secret*. So the meaning is that the Christian, by a life so essentially different from those around him, rather than by reproof in speech, is to 'expose' their sins. (Cf. Wisdom of Solomon ii. 14f.) 'Paul's idea is that of a silent process, comparable to the action of light' (Scott). The use of the word, and the whole thought of the passage, is similar to that of John iii. 20. As light shows up that which is filthy, so the life (and not just the words) of the person who has come to be light in the Lord (verse 8) shows up 'the barren deeds of darkness . . . for what they are' (NEB).

The apostle thinks of the work of grace in the lives of those who do not believe, in three stages—they are exposed, they allow themselves to be manifested, and then they become light. In the beginning their shameful deeds are done in darkness—'they neither see their own baseness, nor think that it is seen by God' (Calvin). But then the light of Christ, shining from the lives of those who have come to know Him, breaks in. Such a coming of the light involves a crisis or judgment (Jn. iii. 19–21). If men hate the light, they will try to avoid it, and shun the exposing of their works. But if they allow their lives to be exposed for what they are, they are *made manifest by the light* (cf. 1 Cor. xiv. 24f.). Their whole lives can then be brought to Christ; and when men are prepared to submit to His scrutiny and dealing, then in His mercy they become light. The darkness is swept away 'and everything thus illumined is all light' (NEB). This is the goal, as verse 8 has put it already —men not only receive the light, but become luminous. Such is the work of Christian evangelism, the light of one soul making another light. The AV translation *whatsoever doth make manifest is light* depends on taking the participle (*phaneroumenon*) as a middle voice, which is without parallel in the New Testament, and particularly unlikely here as the same form has just been used for the passive, and the passive in fact gives a much stronger sense to the whole passage.

14. There follows now a relevant quotation, the substance of which is scriptural (Is. ix. 2, xxvi. 19, lii. 1, lx. 1), but whose words do not correspond precisely to the Old Testament. Their form (in that they refer to the work of 'Christ') prevents our thinking that they might be an otherwise unrecorded saying of the Lord Himself. The most likely explanation is that we have here another little fragment of an early Christian hymn (see on verse 19). It might well be from a baptismal hymn, since coming to Christ and being baptized were spoken of as enlightenment (cf. Heb. vi. 4, x. 32). 'It is significant' also, Bruce points out, that the 'precise rhythm' used here 'was specially associated with religious initiation-chants', so that there is some real possibility in the suggestion that 'Christians took the rhythm over for use in the act of Christian initiation'. In it three metaphors for turning to God are linked—awaking from sleep, being raised from the dead, and going out of the darkness into the light. The challenge to awake from the sleep of carelessness and sin comes similarly in Romans xiii. 11, the passage that led to Augustine's conversion (cf. 1 Thes. v. 6f.). The beginning of chapter ii has already described sin as spiritual death, and shown that Christ's gift is nothing less than new life. The symbolism of light and darkness is the dominant theme of these verses. The verb used here is *epiphauō*, equivalent to *epiphauskō*, used in the LXX of Job xxv. 5 and xxxi. 26 of the sun or moon shining forth, and *epiphōskō* used in Matthew xxviii. 1 and Luke xxiii. 54 of the new day dawning. So it is best to take it as the RV, 'Christ shall shine upon thee.'

d. Wisdom to replace folly (v. 15-21)

15. The apostle has spoken of the sins of the heathen life which must be renounced, and in doing so he has spoken of forsaking the darkness of that old life, and coming to be light in the Lord. But light is a symbol of knowledge as well as of purity. In Christ his readers have been enlightened. So they must live—again the word *walk* is used (see on ii. 2)—day by day, *not as fools, but as wise*. Wisdom has been given (i. 8), and they can pray in all things for the spirit of wisdom (i. 17). So they must display in their lives the wisdom of God (iii. 10). As the context shows, and as Paul puts it in the parallel in Colossians iv. 5—'walk in wisdom toward them that are without'—his particular thought was of their life before the eyes of the non-Christian world. The AV *circumspectly* is probably not correct here. In different MSS the adverb *akribōs* is in different positions. AV translates those MSS where it is next to the verb *walk* and after the conjunction *pōs* (RV 'how'). The more likely reading is that which has it before the conjunction, and thus we have RV, 'look therefore carefully how ye walk', and Moffatt, 'be strictly careful then about the life you lead'. 'He bids them keep a close watch on the principles by which they are regulating their lives' (Murray). This is a command that is essentially more likely to come from Paul's pen than that they should walk 'precisely' or 'strictly'. Paul could well use this word in its superlative form of his former life as a Pharisee (Acts xxvi. 5), but to use it of the Christian life would have conveyed too much of a suggestion of renewed legalism.

16. Once again he is very practical. Walking in wisdom involves in particular the right use of time, and not just the space of time to work for God that each day offers (for which the Greek *chronos* would have been used), but the fit time, the God-given opportunity (*kairos*—see on i. 10). Galatians vi. 10 is parallel, 'As we have therefore opportunity, let us do good unto all men.' 'Buying up the opportunity' RV mg. translates our verse here. The verb used is *exagorazō*, meaning literally 'buying from'. It has the sense of 'redeem' in Galatians iii. 13 and iv. 5, but the prefix *ex-* may have simply an intensive force, and perhaps the word has lost its connections with marketing, and simply means 'use . . . to the full' (NEB). Paul adds the reminder that *the days are evil*, and so shows he is aware of the great pressure in the direction of misuse of time and opportunity. The Christian must not relax but overcome that pressure in his own life, and use every chance to turn others from darkness to light. There may also be the suggestion that because the days are evil, they are under God's judgment, and for that reason 'the time is short' (1 Cor. vii. 29), and each opportunity must be taken before it is too late.

17. He repeats that they must not be *unwise*, this time using *aphrones*, a word that suggests not so much a lack of essential wisdom (as does *asophoi* in verse 15) as a moral stupidity in action. Once again he uses the verb that strictly means 'become', implying the possibility of slipping back from the integrity and good sense with which they have begun to act. Their earnest quest each day, if they are to buy up their opportunities, is to have *understanding*, and the most practical and needful thing to be understood is *what the will of the Lord is*. Verse 10 has already spoken of 'proving what is well-pleasing unto the Lord' (RV). Romans xii. 2, as we have seen, combines both expressions in saying 'that ye may prove what is that good, and acceptable, and perfect, will of God'. Thus Paul repeatedly presents this seeking to know, understand and thus to do the will of God as a priority for the Christian's daily walk.

18. A particular and indeed prominent manifestation of the folly of the old life is drunkenness. Right down the ages, as literature from the earliest period onwards bears testimony, man has sought to rise above his cares and gain a sense of exhilaration and gaiety through intoxicants. Scripture never demands total abstinence from intoxicants (except in the case of those who had taken special vows), and that must be a question left to the individual conscience, but it often speaks against drunkenness. It was a danger in the Church of New Testament days, even among those who might be chosen as leaders, as 1 Timothy iii. 3, 8 and Titus i. 7 and ii. 3 show. The specific objection here to being *drunk with wine* is that it involves what the AV translates *excess* and RV 'riot'. The word *asōtia* involves not only the uncontrolled action of the drunken man (compare the use of the word in Tit. i. 6 and 1 Pet. iv. 4), but also the idea of wastefulness. Hence NEB 'dissipation'. The corresponding adverb is used in the familiar phrase 'riotous living' in the parable of the prodigal son. Both the wastefulness and the lack of self-control implied by this word are things which should not be seen in the lives of those who have found in Christ the source and the way of wisdom.

But again the apostle is not merely negative. He does not seek simply to take away joy and pleasure from men's lives. He would replace them by a higher and a better. It is no mere coincidence that in Acts ii also the fullness of wine and the fullness of the Spirit are set side by side. There is the implication there, repeated here, that the Christian knows a better way than by wine of being lifted above the depression and the joyless monotony of life, a better way of removing self-consciousness and quickening thought and word and action than by the use of intoxicants. It is by being *filled with the Spirit*.

There is a certain strangeness about the construction in the Greek here that has led the RV to give the alternative translation in the margin, 'be filled in spirit'. Usually the Greek New Testament has the genitive case after the verb or adjective used to describe the filling of the Holy Spirit. (This is the case in Acts ii. 4, iv. 31, ix. 17, xi. 24 and xiii. 52.) The preposition 'in' (Gk. *en*) is unusual, though not impossible, as Acts i. 5 shows when it speaks of being baptized 'in the Holy Spirit' (RV mg.). Romans viii. 9 speaks of being 'in the Spirit' to describe the Christian's experience, as against the non-

Christian's life which is still 'in the flesh'. Ephesians, moreover, gives a special significance to this phrase 'in the Spirit' (ii. 18, 22, iii. 5, vi. 18) as well as to 'in Christ'. It is as if the two thoughts of being filled with the Spirit, and living a life 'in the Spirit' (see on ii. 18), are being expressed at the same time; and this may be assisted by the fact that the little preposition *en* in the New Testament can often have a meaning equivalent to 'with', and also by *en* being used with the relative in the preceding clause. To take the expression as meaning merely to be filled in spirit would be to deprive it of the force of meaning that it clearly has in the context, and indeed how can the Christian be filled in spirit but by the Holy Spirit of God? Finally the tense of the verb, present imperative in the Greek, should be noted, implying as it does that the experience of receiving the Holy Spirit so that every part of life is permeated and controlled by Him is not a 'once for all' experience. In the early chapters of the Acts of the Apostles it is repeated a number of times that the same apostles were 'filled with the Holy Spirit'. The practical implication is that the Christian is to leave his life open to be filled constantly and repeatedly by the divine Spirit. So NEB 'let the Holy Spirit fill you'.

19. Instead of the expression of drunkenness in *asōtia*, there should be an exhilaration of the Spirit expressed in song and praise. In the light of the sequence of this verse it has been suggested that the drunkenness referred to was a feature even of Christian assemblies (1 Cor. xi. 20f. is compared). But neither the drunkenness nor the use of song need be given such a limitation. AV translates, giving the more usual meaning of the pronoun, *speaking to yourselves*, but RV is more likely to be the intended meaning 'speaking one to another', and in iv. 32 we have already had the same meaning of the Greek reflexive (cf. Col. iii. 16). The fullness of the Spirit will find manifestation in fellowship whenever Christians are found together, and will be given joyful expression in song and praise. The *psalmos* was originally that which was sung to the harp, and here perhaps includes not only the psalms of the Old Testament, but those (like Lk. i. 46–55, 68–79 and ii. 29–32) which were songs of the new, but in the spirit and manner of the old psalms. The *humnos* in classical Greek was a festive lyric in praise of a god or hero. We have already seen in this Epistle possible evidence of early Christian hymns (iv. 4–6 and v. 14), and we may have other such fragments in 1 Timothy i. 17, ii. 5f., vi. 15f.; 2 Timothy ii. 11–13; and Revelation iv. 11, v. 13 and vii. 12. It is doubtful whether we should press a distinction between the *hymns* and *spiritual songs*. Every expression of Christian joy is welcomed, and all should come from the *heart*—in fact the melody may sometimes be in the heart and not expressed in sound—and go forth addressed *to the Lord*. A number of New Testament passages like this (e.g. Acts xvi. 25; 1 Cor. xiv. 26; Col. iii. 16; Jas. v. 13) indicate the place of song in the early Church; in the second century Pliny and Tertullian give the same testimony. Singing has always had a great place in the Church's life and worship, and every new movement of the Spirit has brought a fresh outburst of song.

20. Whether in song or in other ways the Christian, the apostle instructs, should constantly be *giving thanks*. Repeatedly, as we have seen (on i. 16), he gives this instruction, and his own writings, as doubtless all his life, are an example in this. So he has a right to tell others to give thanks *always*, and *for all things*, since he himself could give thanks even for weaknesses and afflictions and persecutions (2 Cor. xi. 18ff., and xii. 5ff.). *God the Father* is the Source of all blessing, and thus to be Himself blessed (cf. i. 3), but this is rightly *in the name of our Lord Jesus Christ* because every blessing comes to us through Him, and our praise and thanksgiving go to the Father through Him and in His name.

21. In this verse there is an unexpected, but not illogical, turn in the apostle's exhortation, and one that leads him into the instructions that follow in the whole of the next section, v. 22–vi. 9. He has implied in verse 19 that the enthusiasm that the Spirit inspires is not be expressed individualistically, but in fellowship. He has seen the dangers of individualism in a Christian community, and in 1 Corinthians xiv. 26–33 he corrects this (cf. also Phil. ii. 1ff. and iv. 2). He knew from experience that the secret of maintaining joyful fellowship in the community was the order and discipline that come from the willing submission of one person to another (cf. Eph. iv. 2, 3). Pride of position and the authoritarian spirit are destructive of fellowship. The importance to Paul of the whole concept of submission is evident from the use of the word more than twenty times in his Epistles. He is to apply this in special instances in the next section, but we should note that he first gives it a completely general application. There must be a willingness in the Christian fellowship to serve any, to learn from any, to be corrected by any, regardless of age, sex, class or any other division. Undoubtedly the true reading here, though the phrase is unique in the New Testament, is 'in the fear of Christ' (RV), rather than the AV *in the fear of God*. 'The fear of the Lord' is a great principle of life enunciated again and again in the Old Testament. For the Christian this remains unchanged (2 Cor. vii. 1; 1 Pet. ii. 17), but he knows God in Christ, is called to Christ's discipleship, and his whole life is 'in Christ'. So all human relationships, as Paul will now show, find their pattern and meaning and ordered expression under the authority of Christ (cf. 2 Cor. iv. 5). The most vital of these relationships are those of the family, for in every age the home must be the place where above all the peace and harmony, the love and discipline of Christ are most clearly manifest.

V. RELATIONSHIPS (v. 22–vi. 9)

a. Husbands and wives (v. 22–33)

22. In dealing now with personal relationships, Paul begins with that which is basic for the home, between husbands and wives. It is significant, as Moule points out, that throughout this section husbands and wives are reminded of their duties and not their rights. In the case of wives the duty is that of submitting themselves to their husbands (cf. 1 Cor. xi. 3; Col.

iii. 18; Tit. ii. 5; 1 Pet. iii. 1f.). There is no verb in the Greek original here, but the whole structure of the verse depends on the participle in verse 21. The New Testament throughout emphasizes the dignity of womanhood, and it is an indisputable fact that the example and teaching of Christ have lifted woman in one country and society after another to a position that she did not occupy before. Whereas in many great religions, not least in Judaism and Islam, woman has a far lower place than man, the New Testament emphasizes that man and woman have a perfect spiritual equality (Gal. iii. 28). Moreover, as we see most notably in 1 Corinthians vii. 3–5, Paul also 'pleads for a true mutuality in the physical sex relation' (Allan). Nevertheless in the family, for its order and its unity, there must be leadership, and the responsibility of leadership is that of the husband and father, and his authority must be accepted. When the apostle adds the little phrase *as unto the Lord*, he does not imply that the relationship of wife to husband is directly comparable to her relationship to her heavenly Lord, but rather that when a duty is performed 'in the Lord' (as the parallel passage in Colossians iii. 18 puts it), it is carried out *as unto the Lord*. (See also vi. 1 and 5.)

23, 24. The man's place in the family is one of leadership, and hence authority, to be qualified by the highest demand for love in the verses that follow. But the apostle does much more than present the wife's duty as one to be carried out 'as unto the Lord'. Husband and wife are to see their relationship as following the pattern of the relationship between Christ and His Church. *The husband is the head of the wife, even as Christ is the head of the church.* In the rest of the section the apostle uses one to illustrate the other, backwards and forwards. He uses the marriage relationship to illustrate the deep spiritual relationship of love and dependence, of authority and obedience between Christ and His Church. As Allan puts it, 'Marriage supplies an image of the relationship of the Church to Christ more adequate than the image of the Temple to its Foundation Stone, or even than the image of the Body and its Head. Here we pass from imagery taken from the inanimate or the biological realm to imagery taken from the most fully personal realm.' There is, of course, an Old Testament background to this in the way that the prophets regarded the Lord as Husband of His people, entering into a marriage covenant with them, and loving them with steadfast love, even when, because of their idolatry, they were like an unfaithful wife who had committed adultery (e.g. Is. liv. 1–8, lxii. 4f.; Je. iii. 6–14, xxxi. 32; Ezk. xvi, xxiii; Ho. i–iii). Our Lord in His parables used and extended the application of the same analogy (e.g. Mt. ix. 15, xxii. 2–13, xxv. 1–10). On the other hand the marriage relationship is infinitely ennobled by its comparison with the relationship between Christ and His Church. When it is said that Christ is Head of the Church (cf. i. 22f.; Col. i. 18; cf. also 1 Cor. xi. 3), two things are implied: the responsibility He accepts for the Church, and the Church's responsibility towards Him. There are comparable implications in the marriage relationship.

The apostle, however, cannot limit himself to this description of the relation of Christ to His Church, as Head of the Body. He must add further *he is the saviour of the body*. Perhaps he wishes to imply that there are limitations to the analogy that he has just presented. In the light of the following verses, however, we may ask whether he is not rather beginning to express another part of the analogy. The sacrificial concern of the Lord for the salvation of the Church should have a parallel, even if at a much lower level, in the loving and sacrificial concern of the husband for the welfare of his wife. He is 'the protector of his wife' (Bruce).

But before this point is developed, he would stress again the wife's duty. It needs no argument that *the church is subject unto Christ*; even *so* then, he says, *let the wives be to their own husbands*. The final addition *in every thing* might seem more than can be accepted as God's purpose by this present generation with its stress on the emancipation of womanhood, and the place of woman outside the home in every sphere of life that man occupies. Has not a woman equal rights with a man to self-determination? May not a married woman make herself a career as well as her husband? The answer that the New

Testament would give is that she may do so, provided that it does not mean the sacrifice of the divine pattern for home life, for family relationships and for the whole Christian community. She may fulfil any function and any responsibility in society, but if she has accepted before God the responsibility of marriage and of a family, these must be her first concern, and this is expressed here in terms of her relationship to her husband as head of the home. 'As the Church wholeheartedly devotes herself to Christ, so the wife wholeheartedly accepts her place in the family and devotes herself without reserve to fulfil her function as wife and mother' (Allan). Subject to her husband *in all things* does not mean, however, that she is in the hands of one who has authority to command what he pleases. She is to be submissive to one whose duty to her is expressed in nothing short of the highest demand of self-giving love. Her subjection in the light of this, and in the light of the high ideal of unity that is to be expressed in verses 28–31, is such that 'she can never find grievous or humiliating' (Allan).

25. Now the apostle turns to address *husbands*. Chrysostom puts it, 'Hast thou seen the measure of obedience? hear also the measure of love. Wouldst thou that thy wife should obey thee as the Church doth Christ? have care thyself for her, as Christ for the Church.' The quality of the love the husbands are required to give to their wives is first shown by the word that is used for *love*. Two other words might have been used in Greek for the love of husband for wife, and classical writers would more naturally have used them. There was the word *eraō* that expressed the deep sexual passion of man for woman, and the word *phileō* that was used for affection within the family. Neither of these is used here; instead Paul chooses the typically Christian word *agapaō*, love that is totally unselfish, that seeks not its own satisfaction, nor even affection answering affection, but that strives for the highest good of the one loved. This love has as its standard and model the love of Christ for His Church. It has already been taught as the duty of every Christian in all his relationships (cf. iv. 2, 15f., v. 2). Now it is used to remind husbands that they must not think of what they expect as due to them from their wives, but of what they owe in self-giving and devotion.

26, 27. Typically, Paul cannot refer to what Christ has done in love for His Church without amplifying it. Christ gave Himself even to the death of the cross *that he might sanctify and cleanse* His Church. Such was the purpose of His sacrifice (cf. Heb. x. 29, xiii. 12). We often distinguish between justification as an act and sanctification as a process. Sometimes the New Testament may permit this. The tense of the participle here, translated accurately by RV 'having cleansed', might suggest this in the present instance—first cleansing, then sanctification —but in fact the first verb is an aorist in the Greek, indicating a single act rather than a continuing experience. A number of times in the New Testament sanctification is spoken of as an act accomplished in the past as much as justification or forgiveness (cf. 1 Cor. i. 2, vi. 11; 2 Tim. ii. 21; Heb. x. 29). The two words used here describe two aspects of the same experience; Christ's work is to 'cleanse from the old, and consecrate to the new', and 'in time the two are coincident' (Robinson).

Two agencies are described as making possible the cleansing. It is *with the washing of water*, and it is *by the word*. How does the washing of water, the Christian sacrament of baptism, help to effect sanctification, and the cleansing of the heart from sin? The two are connected again in Titus iii. 5. Calvin no doubt gives the true meaning when he says, 'Having mentioned the inward and hidden sanctification, he now adds the outward symbol, by which it is visibly confirmed; as if he had said that a pledge of that sanctification is held out to us by baptism.' Any thought of the external rite itself automatically conveying the inward spiritual grace is excluded by the addition of *by the word*. It is probably the word of the gospel (cf. Rom. x. 8; 1 Pet. i. 25) rather than the word of confession of faith (Moffatt and others) that is meant. Such is the means by which the sanctification becomes effective in men's lives, and that only as it is believed. As John xv. 3 and xvii. 17 express it, the word received cleanses and sanctifies. The apostle is using great

economy of words, and it may be that in every expression he
has the analogy of marriage in mind. Here there may be an
implied reference to the ceremonial bath taken by a bride
before marriage. There is also a Jewish custom that may go
back even to those days, by which, at the giving of the ring,
the bridegroom said, 'Behold, thou art sanctified to me' (see
Murray).

There is a more obvious way in which an analogy can be
drawn between marriage and what Christ seeks to do for His
Church. The reader is called to think of the preparations that
a bride makes for her marriage that she may appear before
her husband in all her beauty. She wants to be seen lovely and
glorious, not having spot, or wrinkle, or any such thing. So the
Church is to appear before her heavenly Bridegroom (cf.
Rev. xxi. 2). But the difference in this case is that she can do
nothing of herself to make herself beautiful in the eyes of her
Lord. Of necessity it is all His work. He must *present it to
himself a glorious church.* She owes 'all her glory to His work'
(Moule, *CB*). She can only be without *spot, or wrinkle,* the
stains of sin, and the decadence of age, through what is
effected by His sanctifying and renewing work. Paul makes
further use of the phrase he has used in i. 4, *holy and without
blemish.* This is the object of our Lord's cleansing work; indeed
in chapter i it is spoken of as the whole purpose and goal of
the work of Christ. It is the goal that Paul kept before him in
his own ministry. In 2 Corinthians xi. 2 he speaks of his 'godly
jealousy' over the Church to 'present' her 'as a chaste virgin
to Christ'. In Colossians i. 28 he speaks similarly of his work,
not simply in terms of bringing men to the knowledge of their
salvation, but of presenting all men perfect in Christ Jesus.

28, 29. Thus the thought and argument go back and forth.
The love of husbands for their wives is to be modelled on the
love of Christ for His Church. The love of Christ and His
desire for His Church are pictured in the preparation of a
bride for her husband. Now he goes on, *so ought men to love
their wives.* Though there is a uniqueness in the application of
verses 26, 27 to the work of Christ for His Church, yet there

seems inevitably the hint that, even if at an incomparably lower level, the husband is to love his wife, not just because of the beauty he finds in her, but to make her more beautiful. Christ sees the Church in all her weaknesses and failures, and yet loves her as His body, and seeks her true sanctification. Even *so* husbands are to love their wives, *as their own bodies*. It would seem that Genesis ii. 24 is already in mind, though it is not quoted till verse 31. And when he says *he that loveth his wife loveth himself*, he is not exhorting the husband to love his wife as an extension of self-love, or because it is to his own advantage. Again the word *agapaō*, used for love, shows that this is not the case. A man should seek his own highest spiritual welfare, and so the highest good of his wife in every way, as united with himself in the marriage bond.

Paul develops this a little further, and comes closer to the terms of Genesis ii. 24 when he says, *For no man ever yet hated his own flesh*. A man's wife, as Moule puts it, is 'in a profound, and sacred sense, part and parcel of his own living frame' (*CB*). A man nourishes and cherishes his own body, Paul says, employing words that he uses in vi. 4 and in 1 Thessalonians ii. 7 for the nurture of children, and showing incidentally that he gives no place to asceticism for its own sake (cf. Col. ii. 23). Such self-love is not wrong. It is the law of life, and the extension of it to similar care for one's life-partner is the law of marriage. But this thought of the intimate care and love that a husband owes and should give to his partner, Paul cannot help but apply back to what is perfectly and more wonderfully true of what *the Lord* does for *the church*.

30. Now, dwelling simply on this spiritual analogy, he says, *For we are members of his body*. In iv. 25 the thought is of Christians being members 'one of another'; in i. 23 and iv. 12 and 16 it is of the Church as the body of which Christ is Head. Here, though the words in the AV *of his flesh, and of his bones* are probably not original, but added under the influence of Genesis ii. 23, the context shows that the apostle's thought at this point is the still deeper one of the intimacy of the Christian's relationship with Christ. The members are part of Him, as the branches are part of the vine in the teaching of John xv. As in the divine purpose the wife becomes part of the very life of her husband, and he nourishes and cherishes her, even so the Lord does to us as members of Himself, part of His own life that He has joined to Himself.

31. Now at last comes the quotation of Genesis ii. 24 that has been influencing all the apostle's thought. This statement from the creation story is the most profound and fundamental statement in the whole of Scripture concerning God's plan for marriage. It has been the ultimate bulwark of the Church against the arguments for allowing polygamy to remain in the societies where she has met it; it is the ultimate argument against promiscuity; it is the ultimate reason against the Church's countenancing the dissolution of marriage by divorce. When our Lord was questioned concerning the legal permission given to divorce, he gave the answer that must still be given. In an imperfect society, in need of such laws, and for the 'hardness of men's hearts', divorce may be allowed, but it is a declension from the divine purpose, and it can never be seen in any other light. The Lord gave no new teaching on the matter, but directed His appeal back to this verse (Mt. xix. 3–9 and Mk. x. 2–12). Prior to marriage a man or a woman has his or her closest bond with parents, and to them owes the greatest obligation. The new bond and obligation that marriage involves transcends the old. Filial duty does not cease, but the most intimate relationship now, and the highest loyalty, is that between husband and wife, and parents only imperil that relationship by trying in any way to come between. There must be a leaving of parents on the part of husband and wife, and a corresponding renouncing of rights on the part of parents.

32. Paul himself, however, in his work as an apostle, was pre-occupied with the thought of the Church prepared as a bride for her marriage, and living as a wife in love and unity and loyalty with her husband. He saw the beauty of the divine pattern and ideal for marriage, and he strove and exhorted husbands and wives to work out that pattern in the stuff of daily living. But to him in his own personal life and work it was above all the highest analogy that he knew for the still more wonderful relation of Christ and His Church, to which he could not help returning again and again. There is literal truth, he would say, to be worked out in every home. But there is also a *mustērion*. This word we have seen used for the great eternal secret of God's purpose for mankind, hidden in the past, but now revealed in Christ (see on i. 9 and see also iii. 3f., 9, vi. 19). It is used more generally in the plural of divine truths (as in 1 Cor. iv. 1, xiii. 2 and xiv. 2), but it is used sometimes in the singular, as here, to denote some particular deep truth of the divine plan which has been revealed (cf. Rom. xi. 25; 1 Cor. xv. 51). The AV *this is a great mystery* is not a very accurate translation. The RV 'this mystery is great', because of what the word 'mysterious' conveys to the modern reader, suggests something that was not in Paul's mind. The sense is 'The truth that lies here, hidden but revealed in Christ, is a wonderful one'. NEB gets it well, 'It is a great truth that is hidden here.' (1 Tim. iii. 16 affords a close parallel to the expression at this point.)[1] Nor should the words that conclude the verse be taken to imply that he had no thought of the literal application of Genesis ii. 24. Westcott says that after speaking of the *mustērion*, 'St. Paul seems to pause for a while and contemplates the manifold applications of the primitive ordinance . . . and then he marks the greatest of all.' *I speak concerning Christ and the church.* They are made one together. The husband's position as head, and his duty of sacrificial love and devoted care for his wife are but pictures, imperfect, but the best that this life can offer, of Christ as Head, and of His love, self-sacrifice and concern for His Church. The dependence of the wife on her husband and her duty of submission are a picture of how the Church should live and act towards her divine Lord.

---

[1] The Latin translation of *mustērion* as *sacramentum* has led to marriage being regarded as a sacrament; but in the usual sense we give to the word 'sacrament' it can hardly be so called, or set alongside the two great 'sacraments of the gospel'.

33. *Nevertheless* the last word must be the practical one on the subject that the apostle had set out to write about. Leaving aside now the analogy to which he has been led, he sums up, that *every one* may take as applying to himself *in particular*, the injunction *let the husband love his wife even as himself*. Love, pure and simple, but transcendent, the truly Christian love (*agapē*) that embraces what is pure in every other love, is the husband's duty. *Reverence* is the wife's duty. The verb here is more literally 'fear' (RV), the same as the noun in verse 21, but that word conjures up in our minds the thought of fearfulness, which is far removed from the true meaning here. Love cannot co-exist with such fearfulness (see 1 Jn. iv. 18), but a deep strong love of wife for husband can be based only on the 'fear' that is both 'reverence' and 'respect'. It is this kind of 'fear' that the Bible so frequently calls on every individual soul to show before God (see on verse 21), and which finds special human application too in the duty of children to parents (Lv. xix. 3), subjects to their rulers (Jos. iv. 14; Pr. xxiv. 21), servants to masters (1 Pet. ii. 18), and now here wives to husbands.

b. Children and parents (vi. 1–4)

1. From the relationship of wives and husbands the apostle now turns to that between children and their parents. The former began with the call to submission, and so here *children* are first exhorted to *obey* their *parents*. Both here and in Colossians iii. 20 the 'honour' of the first commandment is given the specific direction of obedience. Then in a manner typical of this Epistle the apostle adds the phrase *in the Lord*. Its use here is not because the apostle contemplates 'the situation where parental orders might be contrary to the law of Christ' (Bruce), but because it is the Christian home which is in his mind. The Colossians parallel may be taken as interpretative when it says of such filial obedience, 'this is well-pleasing in the Lord' (RV). Even a child in his simple way can know what it means to love *in the Lord*, and to obey for His sake. Then the reason given for obedience is striking in its austerity: *for this is right*. Perhaps his thought is that it is accepted as proper in every society; it is right by the Old Testament law; it is in accordance with the example of Christ Himself (Lk. ii. 51). Or it may be that the form of his expression was intended to carry the reminder that in some things children must accept and follow before they can see all the reasons.

2. The fifth commandment is quoted, essentially as in the LXX of Exodus xx. 12 and Deuteronomy v. 16. As Murray says, 'In the case of the children it was natural to clinch the instruction by a quotation from the Commandments which they must have been taught early.' But, despite his austere statement in verse 1, the apostle does not stop with stating the law that is to be obeyed. There is a *promise* attached to it. It is difficult, however, to be sure what he meant when he said that this fifth commandment *is the first commandment with promise*. It is asked, Does not the second commandment contain a promise too? Or, if the reference there to the mercy of God being shown to thousands of generations is to be regarded as a statement rather than a promise, then is not the fifth the only one of the ten with a promise? Various explanations have been offered. Some have taken 'first' to mean the first in the second table of the Decalogue. But the Jews commonly divided the Ten into two tables of *five* each. There is indeed no need to take the Decalogue as the sum total of the commandments. As Moule puts it, 'The Decalogue is, so to speak, the first page of the whole Law-Book of Revelation' (*CB*). Others take *first* as meaning the first to be learnt by children, and then the words 'with a promise' are added as a reminder for their encouragement. Perhaps, however, especially as there is no article before the noun in the Greek, we should take the meaning as that this fifth commandment is a 'primary commandment'. Matthew xxiii. 23 and Mark xii. 28 speak thus in terms of commandments of prior importance, and it is noteworthy that in Leviticus xix. 1ff. the call to holiness is followed by a statement of various commandments of which this stands first. Thus we take it that this commandment is urged on children as a priority for them, but also as holding out a great promise.

3. In the quotation of the promise there is dependence on Exodus xx. 12 and Deuteronomy v. 16, but the LXX is more freely used, and in particular the reference to 'the land which the Lord thy God giveth thee' is shortened by the omission of the qualifying clause which no longer applied as in Old Testament days. Thus it became more natural to translate *on the earth*. It is not necessary to take the promise in an individualistic sense, or as a literal promise of longevity. Although the singular pronoun was used in the original, it is doubtful if the spiritually-minded, even in Old Testament days, regarded its greatest significance as a personal promise for those who showed filial piety. Then, as in any generation, it could be seen that the strength of family life, and the training of children to habits of order and obedience, were the means and the marks of the stability of a community or nation. When the bonds of family life break up, when respect for parents fails, the community becomes decadent and will not *live long*.

4. As in the case of husbands and wives, not all the obligation is on one side. Parents have their duties, and a warning is necessary for them, and probably when the word *fathers* is used, both parents are in mind, as apparently is the case in Hebrews xi. 23. *Provoke not your children to wrath* is the word for parents. The noun from the verb here, *parorgizō*, has been used in iv. 26, and the verb itself is in Romans x. 19, quoting Deuteronomy xxxii. 21. It is right for parents to demand obedience, but there must not be 'capricious exercise of authority' (Robinson). Discipline is essential in the home; but not unnecessary rules and regulations and endless petty correction by which children are 'discouraged' (Col. iii. 21). The positive duty is expressed in a word used already in v. 29 where it is translated 'nourisheth'. The word was used originally of bodily nourishment, but came to be used for the nurture of body, mind and soul. With its intensive preposition (*ek-*) before it, it suggests 'development by care and pains' (Moule, *CB*). 'Let them be fondly cherished', says Calvin. But all the time, foremost in the parents' minds, is to be not just the harmonious relationships of the home, or the happiness of the children, but their regard for the Lord. The highest duty of parents is to bring up their children *in the nurture and admonition of the Lord*. The two nouns repay closer study. *Paideia* is more than *nurture*. The noun, and its corresponding verb, may have the force of correcting or chastening, as in 1 Corinthians xi. 32, 2 Corinthians vi. 9 and 2 Timothy ii. 25, but may also have the positive meaning of instruction (e.g. Tit. ii. 12). 'Discipline' is perhaps the best translation. *Nouthesia* is more specifically *admonition* or 'correction', and it is used of the purpose of the Old Testament in 1 Corinthians x. 11. In fact it is significant that both words are used to express the purpose of Scripture, and that in 2 Timothy iii. 16 is the only other Pauline use of *paideia*. The NEB well translates 'give them the instruction, and the correction, which belong to a Christian upbringing'. *The nurture and admonition of the Lord* is that which the Lord is able to bring into the life of a child if parents do their work of teaching and training in the Word of the Lord. This is the highest duty of Christian parents. As Dale puts it, 'parents should care more for the loyalty of their children to Christ than for anything besides, more for this than for their health, their intellectual vigour and brilliance, their material prosperity, their social position, their exemption from great sorrows and great misfortunes.'

c. Servants and masters (vi. 5–9)

5–7. Lastly the apostle turns to the relationships between servants and masters. In justice to the original and its setting in the life of the time, it should of course be said that the apostle is still dealing with relationships within the family or household as he writes this section, and that *servants* should be translated as 'slaves'. As Bruce points out, in this Epistle and also in Colossians and 1 Peter 'the injunctions to slaves are more extended than those to masters, and are accompanied by special encouragements', probably thus reflecting 'the social structure of the churches addressed'.[1] But although the numerous slaves who had come into the Christian fold were in the apostle's mind as he wrote these words, the principles of the whole section apply to employees and employers in every age, whether in the home, in business, or in the state. 'The attitude to work and the spirit demanded of masters and those under them are just as relevant in a free society as in a slave economy' (Allan). In the first place there is here another application of the principle of submission that is the keynote of this section. *Be obedient*, servants are told, and the same word is used as in verse 1 in the address to children. Paul's choice of phrase in calling them to render this obedience to those who are their *masters according to the flesh*, immediately brings to their minds the higher Master who is Lord over this relationship. In every case the apostle goes further than we might expect with his demand for submission. Here he does so by adding the phrase *with fear and trembling*. Indeed the thought that dominates the whole section on relationships is that of submission 'in the fear of Christ' (see v. 21). The parallel passage in Colossians iii. 22 enjoins servants to render obedience 'fearing God' (cf. 1 Pet. ii. 18). Murray perhaps is right when he says that 'An element of "fear" enters into all relationships when their essential sacredness is realized.' That sacredness is expressed here (in a way that is paralleled in v. 22 and vi. 1) by the phrase *as unto Christ*. Whatever the Christian does is to be done as to the Lord (Rom. xiv. 7-9), and this is particularly true of the attitude of submission that he is to show towards others.

It means, moreover, the transformation of the Christian's entire standards of work and service into something totally different from the standards of the world. Work and service are to be rendered to an earthly master, as if they were being offered to the heavenly Lord Himself. This would hardly have been easier to accomplish for one who, in Paul's day, was a

---

[1] On the question of the attitude of the early Church to slavery as an institution see Dale, pp. 403ff., and J. B. Lightfoot, *St. Paul's Epistles to the Colossians and to Philemon* (1875), pp. 321ff.

slave against his will, than it would for an employee today, with all the arguments based on materialistic concepts to face. But once again Paul does not merely present a high spiritual ideal and leave it there. He is searchingly practical. He demands that service be given in *singleness of . . . heart*. Honesty of purpose and wholehearted effort must characterize the Christian employee. The same word (*haplotēs*) is applied to both 'secular' work and to the 'spiritual' service of Christians; the New Testament uses it most frequently of liberality in Christian giving (Rom. xii. 8; 2 Cor. viii. 2, ix. 11, 13). The Bible allows no distinction between sacred and secular. *Eye-service* is excluded, and here and in Colossians iii. 22 a word seems to have been invented by the apostle to express his thought. Service 'under the compulsion of inspection' (Moule, *CB*) should not so much as be considered by the Christian. If the aim of employees is to be *men-pleasers*, they will give service only in the things that are seen by men. The Christian's ideal is for his daily work, seen or unseen by men, to be accepted as *the will of God*, rejoiced in, and done not by constraint or carelessly but because it is His will. Christian employees are *servants*—even 'slaves'—not merely of men, but *of Christ*. So all service is to be rendered, the apostle repeats, *as to the Lord, and not to men*. 'The conviction of the Christian workman is that every single piece of work he produces must be good enough to show to God' (Barclay). In everything the spirit of the work, and not merely the output as man sees it, is what matters—what is done, is to be done *from the heart* and *with good will*. Then a man will give loyal service and give his very best to his master whatever attitude his master takes to him.

8. Finally in these instructions to servants the eye is turned to the future reckoning. The New Testament often thus gives the double incentive. Worthy service is to be given as to the Lord who even now is Witness of all that is done. But also it is to be remembered that *of the Lord* a man shall *receive* whatever good, or bad, he has done. Both good and bad are mentioned in the parallel Colossians iii. 24f., and in 2 Corinthians v. 10 and in the Lord's parables of judgment, such as those in Matthew xxv. But only good is mentioned here, since the apostle's purpose at this point is encouragement rather than warning. He knows what it will mean to his readers who are slaves to live out what he has said. So he reminds them that nothing is unwitnessed by the Lord in heaven, nothing well done is ever done in vain. There may be no thanks on earth. A man may reap only criticism and misunderstanding. But he can know that there is an unfailing reward for faithful service (cf. Lk. vi. 35; 1 Pet. i. 17; Rev. xxii. 12). We should not feel that there is any contradiction between this teaching of reward and that of justification by faith alone. In the absolute sense a man who has done all his duty can only describe himself as an 'unprofitable servant' and whatever reward he receives as a gift of grace. Also it is true that from the self-centred life, that is without repentance and faith and their fruits, there can come no service rendered as to the Lord from the heart, that He can reward.

Finally, as a link between verse 8 and verse 9 the words are added, *whether he be bond or free*. This principle, like everything else that can be said of man's duty before God and God's judgment of man, applies to all alike, rich and poor, slave and free, servant and master. But it is to masters that the apostle must now speak.

9. *Do the same things* to your servants, he says to the masters, thus making it clear that the same principles apply to them also. The outward actions required may be very different, but there is the same need to act towards servants 'as to the Lord', as doing 'the will of God', as showing 'good will', in fact, as servants have been called to act towards them. 'Consult their good as you expect them to consult yours' is the way that Moule paraphrases (*ES*). Then a very practical point is touched on. *Threatening* came very easily to the lips of the master of slaves in the ancient world, and the slave could not answer back. The employer may still today speak and act as the one who has the 'whip-hand'. But the Christian master is reminded that all that he says or does to his servant must be said or done remembering that he has a Lord and *Master* . . .

in heaven. To Him he must give account, and not least of the way that he has treated those who have had to call him 'master'. RSV accurately translates here, bringing out Paul's point that both servant and master stand ultimately on the same level, 'he who is both their Master and yours is in heaven, and . . . there is no partiality with him'.[1] To Him both must give account. He watches over the relationship between them (cf. Jas. v. 1ff.). Servants have been told to render all their service as to their heavenly Lord. Masters are told to act towards their servants bearing in mind the fact that they are themselves servants, and the heavenly Master is the One to whom they must give account. They have, moreover, the example that He Himself set 'in the days of his flesh' for all in positions of authority to follow (Jn. xiii. 13ff.).

VI. CONCLUSION (vi. 10–24)

a. The Christian conflict (vi. 10–20)

10. *Finally, my brethren* the apostle says as he is about to bring his letter to a close. He has spoken of the greatness of the purpose of God in Christ, of the glory of His high calling, and the life that should follow from it. The standards have been set, the standards for personal life, for life in the fellowship of the Christian community, and in the more intimate circle of the home. Yet he wants still to remind his readers that such a life cannot be lived without a spiritual battle, of whose intensity he has become more and more conscious in his own experience. The one paramount necessity in this is the power of God. *Be strong*, he says; or rather, as RV mg. shows, taking the Greek as a passive, 'be made powerful' (cf. Acts ix. 22; Rom. iv. 20; 2 Tim. ii. 1). A person cannot strengthen himself; he must be empowered, and that not once for all but constantly, as the tense of the Greek indicates. Furthermore, he says not 'by the Lord', though that would be true enough, but again *in the Lord*. When life is lived in union with Him, within the orbit

---

[1] RV and RSV both accept a reading that is more likely to be original than that taken by the AV which speaks simply of *your Master*.

of His will and so of His grace, there cannot be failure due to powerlessness (1 Jn. ii. 14). Apart from Him the Christian can do nothing (Jn. xv. 1–5), but there is available all *the power of his might*. This phrase brings us back to two of the words that have been used already in i. 19 (and a third, *dunamis*, is in the verb that he has employed), and the repetition gives the same emphasis on God's resources of prevailing, triumphant power as we noted in that passage.

11. Such strength is needed, for the conflict is fierce and may be sustained. But Paul now expresses in another way the equipping that the Christian needs—it is *the armour of God*, the *panoplia* (cf. Rom. xiii. 12; 1 Thes. v. 8), the sum total of all the pieces of armour (*hopla*) that he will describe in verses 14–17. *The armour of God* might mean that armour that God Himself wears or that He supplies. Perhaps both were in mind. Day by day the apostle, at this time of his confinement (see on verse 20), was in all probability chained to a Roman soldier. His mind must often have turned from the thought of the soldier of Rome to the soldier of Jesus Christ, and from the soldier to whom he was bound, to the heavenly Warrior to whom his life was linked by more real, though invisible, bonds. As we shall see later in more detail, the description of the armour of the heavenly Warrior, as given in Isaiah lix. 17 (cf. Wisdom of Solomon v. 17–20), was in his mind; and Paul would have thought of the correspondence between the weapons of His armour and those given by Him to the soldiers serving in the war under Him. He would have thought too of the other details of the armour of the soldier at his side, and their counterparts in the provision for the Christian's spiritual conflict. These weapons that he is to describe are given that men *may be able to stand against the wiles of the devil. Stand* indeed is the keyword of the passage; for, as Moule puts it, 'the present picture is not of a march, or of an assault, but of the holding of the fortress of the soul and of the Church for the heavenly King'(*CB*). The same word is used for *the wiles of the devil* as has been used in iv. 14 where we saw that it involved the idea of 'cunning devices'. This is the first indication of the difficulty of the fight. It is not just against the strength of man, but against the stratagems of a spiritual enemy, the subtle plans of the enemy of souls of which every experienced Christian warrior is well aware (cf. 2 Cor. ii. 11).

12. The thought of a personal devil, though found in every part of the New Testament (e.g. Mt. iv. 1–11; Jas. iv. 7; 1 Pet. v. 8f.; 1 Jn. v. 18), does not commend itself in all quarters today. Still less does the idea of the *principalities* and *powers* of evil and spiritual *rulers of the darkness of this world*. But we should be slow to reject the biblical terms in which the spiritual life and its conflicts are spoken of, and realize rather that our vastly increased knowledge of the physical universe has not necessarily increased, and may in fact have dulled, our sense of the spiritual. We should be hesitant to regard ourselves as wiser than the apostles and our incarnate Lord concerning the unseen world. As C. S. Lewis and other contemporary writers have shown, the insidiousness of spiritual temptations can hardly be more aptly or more powerfully described than in terms of personal agencies of evil, and indeed their explanation in purely material terms is more than difficult. Modern man feels himself to be up against powers which, even if he describes them in material terms, are beyond his control, in spite of all his ability to penetrate the mysteries of the material universe and bring it into subjection. In any case the apostle in his day would not have his readers underestimate the power of the forces against them. We may bring out the emphasis of the original by translating, 'Not for us is the wrestling against flesh and blood.' Momentarily he would change from the figure of a soldier armed for battle to that of a wrestler; for the latter gives the stress he seeks to convey on the personal nature of the conflict, and the reminder that guile as well as brute strength has to be faced. Then we have a list of synonyms similar to that of i. 21 for the spiritual forces that are the Christian's enemies, but the preposition is repeated with each as if to denote that 'each is to be dealt with severally'. (Westcott). There is one word in the Greek (*kosmokratoras*) for the whole phrase *rulers . . . of this world*. It can be used for one who is the ruler of the whole world, or for one whose authority is in the world, in the sense in which the devil is so described in John xii. 31, xiv. 30 and 2 Corinthians iv. 4. The world is frequently spoken of thus in the New Testament as in the power of the evil one (1 Jn. v. 19), and in consequence in *darkness* (cf. Lk. xxii. 53; Rom. xiii. 12; Col. i. 13). Those who, under the devil himself, hold such power in the world, and in consequence keep men in darkness, are those against whom Christians have to do battle. They are the 'spiritual powers of wickedness'—a more accurate translation than the abstract *spiritual wickedness* of AV—and against them the Christian is engaged in *spiritual*, not physical, conflict. Indeed as his own life has been described as raised above this material world to 'the heavenly places' where he lives 'in Christ' (ii. 6), so his spiritual conflict is there, and it is his spiritual possessions there (i. 3) of which the powers of evil would try to rob him.

13. *Wherefore*, Paul says, as you realize the grim power and resources of our spiritual foes, *take unto you the whole armour of God*. Only at great peril can it be neglected. Three times he repeats now the word that has been used in verse 11, when he says that the great objective of the Christian warrior is to be able to *stand*. In fact the first use of the word in this verse is in the compound verb *withstand* (*antistēnai*; the simple verb is *stēnai*), implying a stand against great opposition (cf. Jas. iv. 7 and 1 Pet. v. 9, where the same word is applied to the same spiritual conflict). *The evil day*, to which particular reference is made, indicates a time when the conflict will be most severe, due both to persecution from without and trial from within the Christian fellowship. The apocalyptic passages of the Gospels (e.g. Mk. xiii. 4–23) and Paul in his Epistles (e.g. 2 Thes. ii. 3) alike refer to the quickening of the conflict, the increase in intensity of the warfare, in a great crescendo, before the 'day of the Lord' comes (cf. 1 Jn. ii. 18f.). For this in particular, as for every lesser 'evil day', the Christian must be prepared. There are many things to be done in the Christian's life, many opportunities of service, but Paul could see the possibility of a person doing great things, even the works of an apostle, and yet being a castaway in the end (1 Cor. ix. 24–27). So he stresses here with all the emphasis he can, that *having done all*, having accomplished great things (as the verb implies), they must be sure to *stand*.

14. *Stand therefore*, he says, in the armour provided, which alone will make you invincible. The RV 'having girded your loins with truth' is more accurate than the AV, and similarly in the translation of the next two participles. It shows the tense better, and conveys the sense of a deliberate personal action that the Greek participles indicate. The order in which the pieces of armour are described is the order in which the soldier would put them on. Strictly the girdle is not part of the armour, but before the armour can be put on, the garments underneath must be bound together. The metaphor of girding is so often used in the Bible because it describes a preparatory action necessary for a person with the flowing garments of those days before work could be done, a race run, or a battle fought (e.g. see Lk. xii. 35; 1 Pet. i. 13). Isaiah lix. 17 and the description of the Christian's armour in 1 Thessalonians v. 8 do not mention the girdle, but Isaiah xi. 5 says of the 'rod out of the stem of Jesse' that 'righteousness shall be the girdle of his loins, and faithfulness the girdle of his reins'. We may conclude that it is not the truth of the gospel that is alluded to, but the undergirding of truth in the sense of integrity, 'truth in the inward parts' of which Psalm li. 6 speaks. As 'the girdle . . . gives ease and freedom of movement', so 'it is the truth which gives this freedom with ourselves, with our neighbours and with God. Lack of perfect sincerity hampers us at every turn'.[1]

Secondly, there is *the breastplate of righteousness* which must be 'put on' (RV). This description comes from that of the heavenly Warrior in Isaiah lix. 17, and this fact, as well as the reference of 2 Corinthians vi. 7 to 'the armour of righteousness on the right hand and on the left', seems to indicate that what was in the apostle's mind at this point was not the righteousness of God which is imputed to us (Rom. iii. 21f.), that means our

[1] H. L. Goudge, *Three Lectures on the Epistle to the Ephesians* (1920), p. 76.

justification and the forgiveness of our sins; but, as Calvin, Westcott, Moule and many others take it, uprightness of character, 'loyalty in principle and action to the holy law of God' (Moule, *CB*). To neglect what we know to be a righteous action is to leave a gaping hole in our armour. We may compare this use of the word *righteousness* with that in v. 9 and in Romans vi. 13 and xiv. 17.

15. Thirdly, Paul says 'having shod your feet with the preparation of the gospel of peace' (RV). The word translated *preparation* can have two quite different meanings. It may be 'preparedness', and some, taking this as the right meaning here, assume that although defence is primarily in the apostle's mind in his description of the Christian conflict in this passage, he cannot just think of the Christian defending himself. He must go forward with the gospel. Part of his necessary equipment, therefore, is the readiness at any moment to take out the good news of peace to others. It has been argued that the apostle's thought has moved from Isaiah lix to Isaiah lii. 7, which was in his mind in ii. 17. Another meaning of the Greek noun *hetoimasia*, however, is 'preparation' in the sense of a 'prepared foundation', and thus it appears to be used in the Greek of Psalm lxxxix. 14 (lxxxviii. 15 in LXX). This would give the meaning here that the knowledge of and dependence on the gospel that gives a man peace in his heart and life is a necessary equipment (like the hobnailed sandals of the Roman soldier) if he is to have a firm foothold in the conflict. So NEB: 'let the shoes on your feet be the gospel of peace, to give you firm footing.' This second meaning fits the context better, with its dominant thought of being able to stand unmoved against the foe. Even so the words used carry the hint that warfare is not the complete description of the Christian's occupation—he is also a messenger with good news. There is also a beautiful paradox, that even in the midst of great struggle, the Christian has inner peace (Jn. xvi. 33); he is fighting against evil within and without, but with this purpose that nothing may prevent his taking the gospel of reconciliation and peace to the world.

16. Next, 'to cover all the rest' (Scott), comes the *shield*, and the word used is that which describes the large *scutum* which in effect did cover much of the body. The *shield* is *faith*, by which—as in 1 Thessalonians v. 8 when Paul speaks of 'faith and love' as the breastplate—he means reliance on God. 'The true safeguard in the evil day', Moule says, 'lies ever, not in introspection, but in that look wholly outward, Godward, which is the essence of faith (see Ps. xxv. 15)' (*CB*). A glimpse of the enemy is again thought necessary. In New Testament times darts were often made with tow dipped in pitch and then set on fire, and the wooden shield needed to be covered with leather so as to quench them quickly. The 'wiles of the devil' Paul knew to include such *fiery darts*, the arrow tongues of men, the shafts of impurity, selfishness, doubt, fear, disappointment, that are planned by the enemy to burn and destroy. The apostle knew that only faith's reliance on God could quench and deflect such weapons whenever they were hurled at the Christian.

17. *Take the helmet of salvation*, Paul says next, and the verb used is especially appropriate to salvation as a gift of God (Barry). It implies also that *salvation* is a provision for man that can as definitely be received as any other part of the Christian armour—the soul's deliverance is not a matter of uncertainty to the end. In Isaiah lix. 17 the divine Warrior wears the helmet of salvation as the Worker and Bringer of salvation. For the Christian, salvation is part of the defensive armour that is essential for his safety in the fray. It may be taken as God's gift of salvation from the penalty of sin, but even more as His saving help to protect from the power of sin, and the parallel in 1 Thessalonians v. 8 suggests that here also we may take it to include 'the hope' of final deliverance from the very presence of sin. Without that hope to fortify, without the present deliverance, and the confidence of rescue from the bondage of the past, the Christian may easily be mortally wounded in the conflict.

Finally there is *the sword of the Spirit*. The Old Testament often refers to speech as a sword. The words of wicked men are said to wound as a sword (e.g. Pss. lvii. 4, lxiv. 3). But in the Bible God's own word is also as a sword in His hand, a sword that lays bare, separating the false from the true (Heb. iv. 12), bringing judgment (Is. xi. 4; Ho. vi. 5), but also bringing salvation. His word can thus be wielded by His messengers in the lives of others (e.g. Is. xlix. 2), but here the thought is of the word of God as a defensive weapon for the person who holds it. The genitives in the preceding verses have been genitives of apposition, and some have taken this here to mean that the Spirit Himself is the sword. Clearly, however, what the sword stands for is explained, not by the genitive, but by the following clause. The word is the Spirit's sword,[1] because given by the Spirit (cf. iii. 5; 2 Tim. iii. 16; Heb. iii. 7, ix. 8, x. 15; 1 Pet. i. 11; 2 Pet. i. 21), and it is 'as He works in the believer as the Spirit of truth (Joh. xiv. 17) and faith (2 Cor. iv. 13) He puts the sword into his grasp and enables him to use it' (Moule, *CB*). The Lord's use of the word of Scripture in His temptations (Mt. iv. 1–10) is sufficient illustration and incentive for the Christian to fortify himself with the knowledge and understanding of 'the word' that he may with similar conviction and power defend himself by it in the onslaughts of the enemy.

18. Prayer cannot quite be described as a part of the armour, but the description of the Christian's equipment for the conflict cannot but include reference to prayer. The participle *praying* may in fact be taken with all the foregoing commands. The different parts of the armour have been described, and in effect the apostle would say 'each piece put on with prayer', and then continue still in *all prayer and supplication*. The word *all* or its equivalent is used four times in this one verse in the original. Effective in all its manifold forms, prayer is for every occasion, and to be offered with utter earnestness and constantly for every Christian soul. The New Testament frequently exhorts the Christian not to cease

---

[1] The reference is not only to Scripture, but to all 'words that come from God' (NEB) by His Spirit; we, however, naturally think primarily of the Bible as the *sword of the Spirit*.

from prayer (e.g. Lk. xviii. 1; Rom. xii. 12; Phil. iv. 6; Col. iv. 2; 1 Thes. v. 17), and here the particular point is that every incident of life (*kairos* is the word used—see on i. 10 and v. 16) is to be dealt with in prayer. The apostle is aware that this is no light demand to be made. Man very easily takes his difficulties to his fellows instead of to God. 'The power of prayer is gained by systematic discipline' Westcott wisely says. Constancy in prayer and the natural recourse of the Christian man to prayer come only as prayer has become a habit of life, and as a person has learnt to watch *with all perseverance*. 'Watch' was frequently the exhortation of Jesus Himself to His disciples, and most significantly at the time when they needed to find strength by prayer for their hour of trial in Gethsemane.

But again there is a wonderful balance in Paul's presentation. Even this watchfulness and discipline is not just a matter of human striving; for true Christian prayer is prayer *in the Spirit*. The Spirit is given as Helper, and not least for the task of prayer (Rom. viii. 26f.); but as in the case of the other uses of the phrase in this Epistle (ii. 18, 22, v. 18) *in the Spirit* means more than by the Spirit's help. The Spirit is the atmosphere of the Christian's life, and as he lives in the Spirit grace will be given to watch and power to continue in prayer.

Such prayer, Paul says finally, unlimited in the times and the ways in which it may be offered, is to be unlimited in outreach to those for whom it is offered. The individual Christian is not to think only of his own spiritual conflict, but to be concerned for the whole Church of Christ, and for the victory of all his fellows in the fight (cf. 1 Tim. ii. 1). As Moule puts it, 'The Christian cannot really arm himself with Christ, and use his armour, without getting nearer in sympathy to the brotherhood of the saints of Christ' (*CB*). There is a similar thought in 1 Peter v. 9, where those who are called to resist the devil are reminded that their 'brother Christians are going through the same kinds of suffering' (NEB) 'throughout the world' (RSV).

19. At this point, as Paul has asked prayer for others, he cannot forbear to ask his readers' earnest supplication for him.

As he prayed for the churches, he constantly asked their prayers for him (e.g. Col. iv. 3; 1 Thes. v. 25; 2 Thes. iii. 1). He was aware of his position in the forefront of the battle, even though he was in prison, and of his vulnerability. His great desire was not that they should pray for his liberation, but rather that they should intercede for the great ministry of the word that was his still. Two things he craved for the task: wisdom and boldness. The RV, rather than the AV, is the accurate translation here, 'that utterance may be given unto me in opening my mouth'. ' "Opening the mouth" is an expression used only where some grave utterance is in question', says Abbott. Paul is always conscious of his great responsibility in being entrusted with the gospel of men's eternal salvation, and so he desires above all that whenever he has opportunity to speak that gospel, God will give him the words (cf. Ps. li. 15). Furthermore, as he is aware that by God's grace he has been given understanding in *the mystery of the gospel* (see on iii. 3f. and 9), so he needs constantly to be given power to proclaim it *boldly*, without in any way departing from or diminishing 'the whole counsel of God' (Acts xx. 27, RV), whether for the sake of the praise of men, or to avoid their scorn or opposition. Like the early apostles (Acts iv. 29) his prayer was not for success, nor for deliverance from danger or suffering, but for boldness in proclaiming the gospel of God that was entrusted to him.

20. Up to this point the apostle has said little about himself, except to remind his readers twice that from his prison confinement he is exhorting, pleading, praying (iii. 1, iv. 1). Now, in order to give point to their prayers, he reminds them more specifically of his condition. He is *an ambassador in bonds*. He was aware of the many ambassadors who came to Rome from far and near; he, though in prison at the will of the powerful Roman emperor, felt the dignity and tremendous importance of his position as representative of the King of kings. He was the bearer of the word of his royal Master, the word that entreated men who were at enmity against Him to be reconciled to Him (2 Cor. v. 20). Because of the way that he had thus represented his Lord, he was *in bonds*. This expression *en halusei* probably, though not quite certainly, indicates the manner of his imprisonment. In Acts xxviii. 16 it is said that when Paul first came to Rome he 'was suffered to dwell by himself with a soldier that kept him', and then in verse 20 of that same chapter he tells the Jews that 'for the hope of Israel' he is 'bound with this chain' (*tēn halusin tautēn perikeimai*). He speaks as he does of his imprisonment not to excite feelings of sympathy in his readers; he may desire to inspire and encourage them by the realization that grace has been given to him gladly to bear such imprisonment, but above all he seeks that they should pray for him. Imprisonment brings its own special temptation to bow to the fear of man. He has a responsibility and a privilege too, which remains his to the end of his life. He knows how he *ought to speak* in bearing witness to the gospel. Therefore he repeats the request that they pray that he *may speak boldly*.

b. Final message and greeting (vi. 21–24)

21, 22. The apostle has some final personal words, and these are very closely similar to Colossians iv. 7–9, and in the Introduction[1] we have considered the significance of this fact. If we have rightly judged the whole setting and purpose of this Epistle, the apostle has refrained from personal allusions, either to himself or to his readers, in order to give it a wider usefulness among the churches of Asia. But there are strong personal links that bind him to most of these churches. As by different means he has heard news of them, he would now convey news of his own *affairs* and circumstances. There may have been special need for this because of their anxiety for him (cf. Phil. i. 12), and on account of their temptation to be discouraged by his imprisonment (see on iii. 13). The force of the *ye also* could be that he, having heard of their affairs, was giving them opportunity for their part of knowing his. If, however, he had just written the conclusion to Colossians, he might naturally write in this way, without a moment's thought

[1] See pp. 22f.

whether or not the readers of this letter would be aware of the other that he had written for Colossae.

Tychicus was Paul's messenger, whom he could call *a beloved brother and faithful minister* (see on iii. 7), and he adds now, for the last time in the Epistle, the phrase that conditions all true Christian living and service and relationships, *in the Lord.* Tychicus is the bearer of Colossians and, inevitably, of Philemon too. We first hear of him as one of the representatives of the Asian church who went with Trophimus from Greece and presumably on to Jerusalem at the end of Paul's third missionary journey (Acts xx. 4, and see also xxi. 29). In Titus iii. 12 Paul speaks of sending him or Artemas to Titus, while 2 Timothy iv. 12 refers to him as actually sent to Ephesus from Rome, by which it is implied that he was one of those who served faithfully with Paul in his last trying days. There are traditions, but by no means an agreed tradition, concerning his work as a bishop in later days. The purpose at this time of sending one so close to him as Tychicus was that he might give accurate news, and by that news, and no doubt by other spiritual exhortation, he *might comfort* their *hearts.*

23. There follows a greeting, which like that of the very beginning (see on i. 2) is a true prayer. Paul picks up the three great qualities of the Christian life, the three blessings, of which he has said so much in this Epistle, and prays that his readers may possess them. *Peace*—peace with God, peace in the heart, peace with one another—*be to the brethren.* Then *love with faith.* In one sense love springs from faith, and without faith's union with Christ love cannot begin to grow. Faith in the sense of faithfulness (see on i. 1), however, is a fruit of love. All come *from God the Father*, the Source of all, *and the Lord Jesus Christ*, who is Mediator to us of every spiritual blessing that we can have (i. 3).

24. Now the final prayer is for *grace*, the grace with which the letter began, and which has been the theme of the whole. It is noteworthy that when the word is used in the opening greeting of the Epistles it is regularly without the article in the Greek, but when it stands in a closing prayer the article is used (cf. 2 Cor. xiii. 14; Col. iv. 18; 1 Tim. vi. 21; 2 Tim. iv. 22; Tit. iii. 15; Heb. xiii. 25). Perhaps we should see the influence of the liturgical form of a closing prayer being used even at this time in Christian worship. Perhaps the implication is just that it is 'the grace about which I have said so much'. When he qualifies the *all* who are recipients of grace by the words *them that love our Lord Jesus Christ* it is not with a desire to suggest an exclusiveness of divine grace, but with the reminder that only where there is answering love can the love and grace of God continue to be received in their full and wonderful measure.

The variety of the translations of the word *aphtharsia* reveals the difficulty of determining exactly its meaning. It is used for incorruptibility in the sense of immortality in Romans ii. 7, 2 Timothy i. 10 and elsewhere. Hence RSV 'love undying'. The corresponding adjective *aphthartos* is used in 1 Peter iii. 4 of the 'incorruptible' adornment of character of Christian women, which is at least part way towards the sense of moral 'uncorruptness' (RV) or *sincerity* (see also on iv. 22). Perhaps we need not be pressed to decide between alternatives. What is immortal in nature should be kept uncorrupted in essence. What is spiritual and eternal in the love that God sheds abroad in our hearts by the Holy Spirit (Rom. v. 5) should be kept from every kind of corruption and decay. The love of God is an eternal love, and the love that answers it should be kept up unfailing (1 Cor. xiii. 8), and shine more and more brightly to the perfect day of God.